Following God through Mark

Theological Tension in the Second Gospel

Ira Brent Driggers

Westminster John Knox Press

LOUISVILLE • LONDON

Book design by Drew Stevens
Cover design by Night & Day Design

First edition
Published by Westminster John Knox Press
Louisville, Kentucky

This book is printed on acid-free paper that meets the American National Standards Institute Z39.48 standard. ∞

PRINTED IN THE UNITED STATES OF AMERICA

07 08 09 10 11 12 13 14 15 16 — 10 9 8 7 6 5 4 3 2 1

Library of Congress Cataloging-in-Publication Data

Driggers, Ira Brent.
    Following God through Mark : theological tension in the Second Gospel / Ira Brent Driggers.—1st ed.
        p. cm.
    Includes bibliographical references and index.
    ISBN 978-0-664-23095-1 (alk. paper)
    1. Bible. N.T. Mark—Criticism, interpretation, etc.   I. Title.
    BS2585.52.D75   2007
    226.3'06—dc22
                                                          2007003694

What I know of thee I bless,
As acknowledging thy stress
On my being and as seeing
Something of thy holiness.
—*Gerard Manley Hopkins*

Contents

Abbreviations for English Translations of the Bible

ASV	American Standard Version
GNB	Good News Bible
KJV	King James Version
NAB	New American Bible
NIV	New International Version
NJB	New Jerusalem Bible
NKJV	New King James Version
NLT	New Living Translation
NRSV	New Revised Standard Versoin
RSV	Revised Standard Version

Preface

Readers of this book will easily notice my indebtedness to Donald H. Juel, who, even after his untimely death in 2003, continues to inspire pastors and scholars alike. As many will attest, his zeal for life and for God proved contagious, especially when the topic of discussion was Mark's Gospel. It is my hope, then, that this book captures at least some of that zeal and that it contributes to a vibrant discussion he helped to spark. I would like to have known his response to this work in its finished form, particularly to those places that depart from, and at times challenge, his own interpretation. What I do know is that he would have delighted in the conversation.

Dr. Juel considered biblical exegesis a form of theology, the ultimate goal of which is to say something about God. When my earliest doctoral work on the Markan disciples took me through already well-trodden territory, I followed his lead in exploring the Markan God. What I found, using Karl Barth's well-known phrase, was a "strange new world." There were no substantial and accessible treatments on the subject and, perhaps for that reason, the subject itself proved many times more exhilarating. More significantly, the God of Mark's Gospel proved impossible to pin down. My scholarly inclination to articulate an argument for a single interpretation brought only consternation. Then it occurred to me that perhaps God's mystery is precisely the point. Soon after I began to explore that possibility I discovered, rather ironically, that not all angles on the Markan disciples had been covered after all. There was in fact a theological angle from which the disciples, for all their enigmatic shortcomings, appeared implicated in a divine mystery. Thus my goal became twofold, to describe Mark's depiction of God and the way that depiction comes to bear upon the disciples.

I intend this book for seminarians and senior undergraduates, whether for a class on the Gospel of Mark or on the Gospels in general. Although I quote the Greek text of Nestle-Aland (27th ed.) rather frequently, it is usually parenthetical to my own translation (all translations are my own unless otherwise indicated). I have also kept discussion of method to a minimum (see introduction) so as not to lose focus on the Gospel of Mark itself.

I am extremely grateful to those who read various drafts of this work: Brian K. Blount, Elizabeth Struthers Malbon, Beverly Roberts Gaventa, C. Clifton Black, Matthew L. Skinner, Lynda A. Neese, and Kari C. Foncea. All of them gave insightful and challenging feedback, at times leading to crucial modifications and thus to what I hope is a more nuanced and balanced interpretation. Brian Blount deserves a special word of thanks for his consistently enthusiastic engagement of this project in all its stages. Stephanie Egnotovich, I should also add, was most supportive in her role as editor at Westminster John Knox Press. Of course whatever shortcomings this book contains are strictly my own.

Finally and most importantly I thank my family for their undying support. Thanks to my parents for understanding and appreciating my love for theology and the Bible. Thanks to my two young sons, Harry and Owen, who have yet to understand or appreciate my work and who—for that very reason—add a much needed perspective to its significance. But thanks most of all to my wife, Ingrid, who gave me strength when I needed it most, even when I deserved it the least. I dedicate this, my first book, to her.

Introduction

Following God through Mark

> Their experience is beyond their comprehension because they can-
> not fully grasp what it is they are seeing.
> —*Plato*[1]

The Gospel of Mark tells the story of an incomprehensible God. The actions of this incomprehensible God precede the Gospel's beginning (1:2–3), exceed the Gospel's ending (13:11; 16:6–8), and propel the plot of the Gospel itself. I say "incomprehensible" because while the Gospel tells a story replete with divine activity, its depiction of that activity is predicated upon a profound tension: God acts both through Jesus and apart from Jesus. Moreover, this tension bears directly upon the behavior of characters within the Gospel—most notably Jesus and his disciples—creating various derivative tensions that point ultimately to God's mystery.

These derivative tensions pertain to the disciples' initial following of Jesus, their early misunderstanding of Jesus' miracles, their resistance to Jesus' passion, and, finally, the passion of Jesus itself. In each case the Gospel's hearers receive two irresolvable explanations for why events unfold as they do, explanations that correspond to God's divergent modes of action vis-à-vis Jesus. While God remains the underlying cause of each development, then, the precise logic of divine causation cannot be limited to any single interpretation. The Gospel follows two theological trajectories simultaneously, so that as hearers learn more about God they simultaneously move deeper into God's ultimate mystery. Borrowing the words of Plato, God is "beyond their comprehension because they cannot fully grasp what it is they are seeing."

My analysis follows the progression of the Gospel itself, charting the effects of its developing plot upon a "believing audience" (I define this audience later

1

in the introduction). In chapter one I argue that the Gospel's prologue (1:1–15) generates specific expectations regarding God's role in the narrative—first, that God will function as the narrative's main actor; second, that God will act in two divergent ways in relation to Jesus. On the one hand God will act in and through Jesus, bringing the long-awaited "reign of God" into the world. On the other hand God will act apart from Jesus, speaking from heaven, speaking from Scripture, and, as the audience soon discovers, acting directly upon other characters. I refer to these as God's "invasive" and "transcendent" modes of action, respectively. Together they constitute the Gospel's primary and underlying theological tension; and the narrative will consistently reinforce this tension, though often in surprising ways.

In subsequent chapters I narrow my focus to the way in which God's divergent modes of action impinge upon Jesus' relationship with his disciples. By the word "disciple" I mean the somewhat ambiguous group constituting Jesus' inner circle of followers, a group often represented by "the twelve" (3:14–19; 4:10; 6:7; 9:35; 10:32; 11:11; 14:17–31) and the leaders of the twelve (8:29–33; 9:2–13, 38; 10:28–31, 35–40; 13:3; 14:32–42, 66–72) but that also includes individuals drawn from surrounding crowds (2:13–14; 10:52) along with certain women who "provide" for Jesus (15:40).[2] This focus upon the Jesus-disciple subplot begins in chapter two, where I examine the narrative's first and paradigmatic depiction of the call to discipleship: the encounter between Jesus and the Galilean fishermen (1:16–20). I argue that the narrative's ambiguity regarding the fishermen's response to Jesus allows for two viable, though (logically speaking) mutually exclusive, explanations. On the one hand they follow out of their own volition; yet on the other hand they are, metaphorically speaking, fished by God. The former explanation makes sense of the action as *human* action, while the latter appeals to expectations of *divine* action (particularly God's invasive action in the story). This episode also establishes the audience's vested interest in the fate of the disciples, as Jesus promises their participation in the encroachment of God's eschatological reign ("I will make you become fishers of people," 1:17).

In chapters three and four I divide the bulk of the Gospel in half, maintaining the focus on how God's actions impinge upon the relationship between Jesus and the disciples. In chapter three I concentrate on the first half of the Markan plot (1:21–8:21), noting how the narrative generates expectations for a close alignment between Jesus and the disciples (1:21–4:34) only to thwart those expectations through repeated references to the disciples' fear and misunderstanding (4:40–41; 6:37, 49–50, 52; 8:4, 17–18). It is precisely in this growing rift that hearers discern God's divergent modes of action. For while the narrative gives evidence, on the one hand, of the disciples' sheer dullness in perceiving God's encroaching reign (God's invasive activity), it also suggests, on the other hand, that God has hardened the disciples directly (God's transcendent activity). In other words, their misunderstanding reflects the Gospel's underlying theological tension and thus accentuates the mystery of God.

Chapter four examines the prolongation of this rift in 8:22–15:39. Here, however, the fissure begins to center around Jesus' "necessary" passion (8:31) and its scandalous effects upon the disciples. In the journey episodes comprising 8:22–10:52 this scandal stems from the mere promise of Jesus' suffering, while in the Jerusalem episodes of 11:1–15:39 it stems from the realization of the promise, with the result that Jesus hangs abandoned by his closest followers on a Roman cross. Here too the narrative implicates God in two divergent ways. For in one sense the passion stems from the world's blind and hostile response to God's invasive action through Jesus, in which case the cross is "necessary" in that it is simply inevitable. As Jesus moves closer to Golgotha, however, a different kind of necessity begins to surface, a necessity grounded in God's transcendent action as foretold in the promises of Scripture. Consequently, the disciples' final abandonment of Jesus may be explained in two different ways, both as a self-protective response to violent opposition and, simultaneously, as God's own "scripting" of their actions. As in earlier cases of the disciples' misunderstanding, the narrative sustains both possibilities, creating an experience of tension that points to an underlying divine mystery.

In chapter five I examine the Gospel's conclusion (15:40–16:8), focusing especially on the significance of its perplexing final statement: "And they said nothing to anyone, for they were afraid" (16:8). This abrupt ending, I argue, creates a scenario that jeopardizes the fulfillment of certain key promises, particularly the redemption of the deserting disciples (14:50) and their subsequent fulfillment of Jesus' discipleship teachings. More to the point, it makes the promised continuation of the story an outright impossibility—except insofar as the audience and God are concerned. This makes for a final tension that carries over into the life of Mark's hearers. For in one sense the Gospel's ending commissions them to break the women's silence themselves, to heed Jesus' teachings on true discipleship, and consequently to continue the extension of God's transformative reign into the world. However, that same ending also underscores the alarming fallibility of Jesus' followers and, therefore, the constant need for merciful empowerment from the transcendent God. The Gospel ends on a note of responsibility *and* impossibility, pointing hearers not only to the mystery of God but also to the mystery of discipleship.

PRELIMINARY INTERPRETIVE QUESTIONS

As Hans-Georg Gadamer has duly noted, "To understand meaning is to understand it as the answer to a question."[3] Thus, for the task of biblical exegesis, one's interpretation of a text depends upon the kinds of questions one asks of the text. With respect to the Gospel of Mark, many interpreters have posed questions about its historical accuracy, while others have posed questions about its sources and the religious communities in which those sources originate. Without diminishing the value of these questions, in the present work I pose different ones: How does the Gospel depict God, and what is the significance of this depiction for a believing audience? Yet even these questions imply a number of smaller questions. In identifying these questions and (whenever possible) my answers to them, I hope to lay bare my hermeneutic suppositions while also orienting my work within the field of biblical scholarship.

The Question of God and Theology

My focus on God stems largely from the work of Nils Dahl, who, in a 1975 essay, laments the lack of interest among scholars in a "detailed and comprehensive investigation of [the New Testament's] statements about God."[4] Stated simply, Dahl calls on scholars to pose a particular interpretive question: What does the New Testament say about God? In an era when the theology of the New Testament tends to be defined, in rather broad terms, as its overall message or messages, Dahl insists on a consideration of its theology in the strict etymological sense (*theo*-logy). Throughout the present work I will use the term in this strict sense.

An emerging body of scholarly literature has since begun to heed Dahl's call.[5] More than thirty years later, however, his challenge still echoes over the field of New Testament studies, perhaps most resoundingly in regard to scholarship on the Gospel of Mark. Although a handful of interpreters have begun exploring Mark's God-language, their works are either shorter essays, single chapters, or, in two cases, unpublished dissertations.[6] Thus a comprehensive and accessible treatment of the Markan God has yet to be attempted, and in this respect I hope to advance a still nascent conversation.

The Question of a "Markan" God

My use of the term "Markan" indicates my attempt to read the Gospel of Mark as a distinctive and, in some cases, unique narrative vis-à-vis the other New Testament Gospels. All four Gospels share a significant amount of material, not to mention key fundamental beliefs about, for instance, Jesus' messiahship and his authority to speak for God. Yet in many ways the Gospels also differ from one another, not least with respect to how they portray God.

Over the history of biblical interpretation the differences among the Gospels have often been a source of consternation, particularly when they became an impetus for historical inquiry in the late Middle Ages. Among so many differences, it is often asked, which Gospel has depicted a given event with the most historical accuracy? It is an important question as far as the "historical Jesus" is concerned. In recent decades, however, narrative critics have responded to those same differences with their own equally valid question: What is the meaning or significance of each Gospel as a coherent narrative? With this line of questioning issues of historical background remain relevant (e.g., the realities of first-century Judaism and ancient Greco-Roman culture), particularly if an interpreter seeks to discern what the story meant for an ancient audience. Still, one's primary interpretive question focuses on the meaning of the narrative itself rather than historical events "behind" the narrative—events that the narrative may or may not have depicted accurately.[7] Each Gospel is therefore treated as a coherent story in its own right, bringing its own distinctive perspectives to the larger canonical conversation. In our case it is a distinctively Markan perspective.

In adopting this narrative approach I depart from Dahl in at least one important way, namely, over the question of how one discerns so-called God-language. In his emphasis on "statements about God" and "thematic formulations about God" Dahl reveals an underlying assumption that one understands the New Testament's varying perspectives on God only insofar as he or she understands a limited number of explicitly theological assertions, that is, propositions stating God as an explicit referent.[8] Once one poses the question of Mark's God in terms of the Gospel as narrative, however, the door opens to investigating more subtle literary features such as plot, conflict, irony, and characterization. In this case a portrait of the Markan God emerges not only from highlighting explicitly theological propositions but also, and more fundamentally, from experiencing Mark's Gospel from beginning to end.

In what follows I explain my two primary interpretive foci for gauging this "experience" of Mark's theological narrative. These foci have been discussed at length in Robert Fowler's *Let the Reader Understand*[9] and have been adapted here to my own purposes.

First Focus: Narrative Discourse

Drawing from Seymour Chatman's well-known distinction, I will attempt to focus on the "discourse" that is implied by Mark's "story."[10] This means that I read the story with an eye toward its rhetorical features—"the ways in which the language of the narrative attempts to weave its spell over the reader."[11] Thus I concentrate not merely on the story's content per se but, more precisely, on the way that content functions as communication to the reader and thus shapes the reader.

As one of many potential examples, consider Mark's account of Jesus' baptism: "And just as [Jesus] was coming up out of the water, he saw the heavens torn apart and the Spirit descending like a dove on him. And a voice came from heaven, 'You are my Son, the Beloved; with you I am well pleased'" (1:10–11 NRSV). Close attention to details suggests that only Jesus sees the tearing of the heavens and the descent of the Spirit. We are told that *"he* saw" (not the surrounding crowds, 1:5) and that God speaks only to Jesus (*you* are my Son). It is, in other words, a private revelation.[12]

Attention to the narrative discourse, however, reminds us that although this revelation is "private" with respect to Jesus and God, it never excludes us, the audience. Such an observation may at first seem too obvious even to mention. Yet the interpretive implications cannot be overstated, for it brings to attention how the narrative gives the reader access to certain information that other characters in the story do not have. In this case we "see" and "hear" the same things as Jesus and therefore emerge from the experience privileged, at least with respect to our knowledge, over the surrounding crowds (including, it seems, John the Baptist).[13]

Given that so many characters in Mark's Gospel misunderstand Jesus' words and actions, the privileging of the Markan reader becomes a significant factor in interpretation. The incongruity between the world of characters (who remain largely ignorant) and the world of the reader (who gains crucial knowledge) yields what literary critics commonly refer to as "dramatic irony."[14] As I will argue in subsequent chapters, it is precisely through Mark's ironic discourse to the reader that one understands Mark's story as a story about God.

Second Focus: The Temporal and Dynamic Experience of Reading

In addition to my emphasis on narrative discourse, I will focus on the way the narrative generates a temporal and dynamic experience. This serves as a corrective to what has been called the "spatial fallacy" by which interpreters, faced with a physicality of a written text, objectify it into a thing that "contains" meaning.[15] Such meaning, it is commonly assumed, resides unchanging in the text, waiting to be uncovered by the interpreter.

Such an approach ignores, however, the temporal nature of the reading experience. That is, it overlooks the fact that the reader, in the very act of reading, moves through a host of successive and often divergent experiences, experiences that cannot be synthesized or coalesced into a single, uniform meaning. That is why Stanley Fish, in his seminal essay on "Affective Stylistics," argues that once one highlights the role of the reader, "the report of what happens to the reader is always a report of what has happened *to that point*."[16] The temporal nature of reading excludes the possibility of limiting the task of interpretation to a single, fixed vantage point over against an objectified, spatially conceived text. Stated simply, the spatial fallacy does not account for what actually happens in the act of reading.[17]

Recognizing the temporal nature of reading also means recognizing its dynamic nature since it always involves a variety of experiences succeeding one another in time, some of which may even conflict. That is because narrative often forces the reader to reexamine, and sometimes even to dismiss, assumptions that have been previously confirmed earlier in the reading process. Meaning changes, even though the actual words of the text remain the same.[18] Meaning does not reside statically "in" a text but rather "happens" constantly in relation to the ever-changing experiences of the reader. In this way reading (or hearing) a story is like embarking upon a journey, following what Fowler calls a "meandering path."[19]

A particularly significant example of this occurs in Mark 4:13, when Jesus, having finished his parable of the Sower (4:1–10), asks his disciples: "Do you not understand this parable? Then how will you understand all the parables?" Even at a surface level, the reproach runs against the expectations Mark has heretofore created concerning the disciples. The Gospel's first three chapters cast the disciples in a most positive light, beginning with the call of Simon and Andrew (1:17–18), culminating in the appointment of "the twelve" (3:13–19), and accentuated by the contrasting antagonism of the scribes and Pharisees (2:6–7, 15–16, 18, 24; 3:1–6, 22). Consequently, the introduction of the disciples' misunderstanding at 4:13 forces a significant modification in the reader's viewpoint. The reader now understands what she did not understand before: the disciples, though insiders, can and will misunderstand Jesus.

Mark 4:13 modifies not only the reader's expectations for the disciples but her understanding of previous verses, particularly Jesus' famous parable explanation at 4:11: "To you has been given the secret of the kingdom, but for those outside, everything comes in parables."[20] Prior to the reproach at 4:13 a reader is more likely to hear this explanation simply as confirmation of what she already knows: the disciples are "insiders" while others are "outsiders." With the movement to 4:13, however, such an interpretation is thrown into question. Mark squelches the reader's clear-cut understanding of the disciples by presenting their own misunderstanding of Jesus' teaching. Thus, although the vocabulary of 4:13 may not directly echo 4:12, Jesus' reproach ("Do you not understand?") turns what was once a black-and-white distinction (disciples versus outsiders) into a gray area of incomprehension. Thus the question is immediately raised: What exactly distinguishes the disciples from outsiders?[21]

Questions of Author and Audience

Two important questions remain: Who is "Mark" and who are "Mark's readers"? I have made constant reference to these categories without clearly defining them. To clear up any potential misconceptions, I will explain here how they function in subsequent chapters.

From a historical pespective, the identities of both the original writer and audience are unknown, so that our primary means of reconstructing both parties is the interpretation of the Gospel itself. Consequently, I use the phrases "Mark" and "Mark's readers" to speak of the author and readers *implied* by the narrative. Both the "implied author" and "implied readers" are interpretive constructs, "presupposed by the narrative itself" and, theoretically, "distinct from any real, historical reader."[22] Far from discrediting the task of historical reconstruction, however, these categories simply reframe the question in terms of interpretation, rather than in terms of the history standing behind the text. Particularly in the case of an anonymous Gospel, historical construction stems primarily from interpretation.[23]

Here an important qualification is in order. So as not to commit the spatial fallacy described above, I use the categories of "implied" author and readers as *heuristic* tools, as the means of elucidating my own interpretation of the narrative—but without claiming them as actual narrative "structures" residing "in" the text.[24] I do not presume to reconstruct strictly textual personae apart from my own interpretive assumptions, as if the text per se could simply dictate such a reconstruction. Nor do I presume to know fully where my own interpretive assumptions end and the text's voice begins, assuming that such a distinction can even be made. There is a very blurry line separating ancient from contemporary readers, for while historical reconstruction stems from interpretation, interpretation involves the active engagement of a present-day reader. Again, this does not mean that arguments about the identity of Mark's historical readership have been excluded. It means rather that such arguments are forwarded as acts of interpretation, not as attempts to bypass the narrative in the quest for what lies behind it.

With all of this in mind, then, I offer the following profile of Mark's readership as a necessary component of my overall interpretation. This profile consists of three basic arguments:

1. *Mark's Gospel seeks to address a community of people through oral performance.* Historians of the early church agree that although private and individual reading was possible for those possessing the proper skills, the reading of texts in the first century (and well beyond) constituted a community enterprise whereby a single person read the text—indeed, performed the text—aloud to others.[25] This means that Mark's original audience consisted of hearers, not readers, who would have encountered the Gospel as a temporal and dynamic experience, not as a reified text containing static meaning. Moreover, the likelihood of Mark having been written to edify and instruct early church communities, rather than for the writer's own need to record history, suggests that, even in the present

day, Mark's story is more appropriately experienced in live, communal performance as opposed to silent reading. Even when informed by the insights of reader-oriented criticism, a silent reading will not fully capture the dynamic experience of oral performance.[26] For reasons of both historical accuracy and contemporary suitability, then, I will in subsequent chapters speak of Mark's *audience* (what one might call the narrative's "implied" audience).

2. *Insofar as Mark's Gospel addresses an early church community, it is written to people already predisposed to believe "the gospel of Jesus Christ" (1:1).* It would be inappropriate to venture into a more descriptive definition of this community's beliefs (if it even is a single community) apart from an interpretation of the Gospel itself. By way of anticipation, however, I hold that Mark's audience, as a people of faith, holds a vested interest in Mark's characterization of the disciples and their overall fate in the story. Scholars have long debated the purpose of Mark's troubling characterization of the disciples and the extent to which this characterization distances the audience from Jesus' followers in the story. However, even those who view this troubling characterization as antidisciple polemic would agree that, at least initially, Mark's audience seeks to identify with the disciples in the story—in which case Mark's negative characterization serves to challenge this tendency.[27] By contrast, I will argue that although Mark's rhetoric does produce a cognitive distance between the disciples and the audience, it does not thwart the audience's vested interest in the disciples; rather, it encourages it.

3. *Insofar as Mark's audience consists of those who believe in "the gospel of Jesus Christ," it will lend a great amount of authority to Mark's use of Scripture.*[28] This does not necessarily mean that Mark's historical audience consisted, either wholly or in part, of Jewish believers. It does, however, mean that Mark's narrative implies an audience that shares his reverence for, and faith in, God's ancient promises as recorded in writings such as Isaiah, Malachi, Zechariah, and the Psalms. Borrowing a term from the literary critic Jonathan Culler, one could say that Mark's "ideal" audience, when confronted by Mark's use of Scripture, agrees with Mark that those ancient promises find their fulfillment in the person and ministry of Jesus Christ.[29] Thus, although the Gospel's audience (in any era) can both experience and understand Mark's story without any prior knowledge of Scripture, it will appreciate the theological significance of that story in direct proportion to its familiarity with the Scripture Mark uses to assert God's faithfulness. This point is worth noting in that in the present work I locate many of the Gospel's key theological moments in Mark's allusions to and quotations of Scripture. Indeed, one of the most important of those moments comes in the Gospel's prologue, which is the topic of chapter one.

1

God at/before the Beginning (Mark 1:1–15)

O that you would tear open the heavens and come down, so that
the mountains would quake at your presence.

—Isaiah 64:1

He saw the heavens being torn apart, and the Spirit descending
into him like a dove.

—Mark 1:10

Since narrative generates a temporal and dynamic experience for its audience,
it is appropriate to begin at the beginning, with a discussion of the Markan prologue (1:1–15). Interpreters commonly point to the prologue as the place where
Mark introduces Jesus as the story's main character. To this long-standing interpretation I hope to add a crucial theological dimension. For the same prologue
that creates these expectations concerning Jesus also creates expectations concerning God, namely, that God will function as the story's main actor.
Although Mark will not depict God with a plethora of "traits," he will depict
God as the story's dominant agent of activity.[1] Consequently, in many respects
the actions of human characters in the story may be seen as reactions to what
God is doing, has already done, or, in some cases, is about to do.

How can Jesus function as the story's main character simultaneous to God
functioning as its main actor? This is possible because the prologue generates
the expectation that God will act through Jesus. Drawing largely from the
work of Donald Juel, I will point to specific details in Mark's discourse that
indicate God's invasion of the world through the spiritual possession of the
anointed "Son" (1:1, 11). I call this God's invasive role in the story, by which
Jesus functions not merely as a representative or teacher of God's will but as

11

the bearer of God's very presence, the human agent of God's encroaching eschatological reign. Jesus is literally a man possessed, and therefore driven, by God's Spirit, while characters responding to Jesus respond (unknowingly) to the God who acts through him.

Yet this is not the complete picture. For the prologue also generates expectations that God acts transcendently—by which I mean *apart from Jesus*. God's invasive activity does not exhaust his role in the story, then, but is only one side of a larger tension. Functioning as a kind of theological prolegomenon, the prologue establishes both sides of this tension without attempting to resolve them. Indeed, as I argue in subsequent chapters, the unresolved tension of Mark's theology defines the audience's journey along the meandering path of the Gospel. In this sense, the narrative sustains and reinforces expectations generated at its beginning.

PREPARING THE WAY FOR GOD/JESUS

The audience hears the distinction between Jesus and God in the Gospel's opening verse: "The beginning of the good news of Jesus Christ, Son of God" (1:1). This opening establishes Jesus as the main character, using the terms "anointed" (χριστός) and "Son" (υἱός) to indicate his privileged status by virtue of his relationship to God.[2] Particularly if the verse stands in the tradition of Psalm 2—a coronation hymn describing Israel's king in identical terms (Ps. 2:2, 7; see Mark 1:10)—one finds here distinctively royal imagery. Jesus is the king, or soon-to-be-anointed king (1:10–11), who rules on God's behalf.[3]

While 1:1 establishes Jesus as the Gospel's main character, 1:2–3 introduces God as its main actor. This composite quote from Scripture, which Mark attributes simply to Isaiah, constitutes a divine announcement that sets in motion subsequent narrative events: "See, I am sending my messenger ahead of you, who will prepare your way [Mal. 3:1; Exod. 23:20], the voice of one crying in the wilderness, 'Prepare the way of the Lord; make straight his paths' [Isa. 40:3]."[4] Mark's generalized reference to "the prophet Isaiah" (1:2) strongly suggests that the unnamed speaker here is God ("I am sending"), a connection reinforced by the original context of Mal. 3:1. The immediate emergence of John the Baptist preaching "in the wilderness" (Mark 1:4) therefore suggests the fulfillment of God's scriptural promises. That is, John's ministry of repentance and baptism (1:4–5) prepares "the way of the Lord." God is making things happen.

Closer attention to scriptural allusions reveals yet further theological dimensions to Mark's discourse. For instance, the description of John at 1:6 parallels the description of the prophet Elijah found in 2 Kgs. 1:8, particularly in regard to Elijah's clothing of hair (ἐνδεδυμένος τρίχας καμήλου) and "a leather belt around his waist" (ζώνην δερματίνην περὶ τὴν ὀσφὺν αὐτοῦ). In light of this parallel, it is significant that the prophet Malachi, already quoted directly at 1:2, promises that Elijah will one day return as a vehicle for God's own actions in the last days: "Lo, I will send you the prophet Elijah before the great and terrible day of the LORD comes. He will turn the hearts of parents to their children and the hearts of children to their parents, so that I will not come and strike the land with a curse" (Mal. 4:5–6 NRSV).[5] Indeed, the invocation of Elijah's eschatological significance, via Malachi, is likely the central point of John's ministry. Mark does not describe John's clothing out of some arbitrary sense of fashion, much less out of a concern to record historical facts, but rather as a way of connecting John with God's end-time activity. God has sent Elijah to bring repentance and to baptize, to "turn the hearts of parents to their children and the hearts of children to their parents." Following the logic of Malachi, as well as Jesus' own proclamation (Mark 1:14–15), suggests that the "great and terrible day of the Lord" has drawn near. Again, God is making things happen.

John, however, is more than the fulfillment of scriptural promises. He also predicts the arrival of the one coming after him (1:7), the one whose superiority to John will be made evident by his baptism "in the Holy Spirit" (1:8). Thus, when Jesus appears on the scene immediately after John's prediction (1:9), the audience has every reason to believe that Jesus is the one of whom John speaks. Consequently, the audience must also situate Jesus squarely within the unfolding plot of divine activity, particularly as part of the "way" that John/Elijah prepares. In other words, Jesus too functions as part of the fulfillment of Scripture quoted at 1:2–3. The scenario initially anticipated in general terms, as God's messenger preparing the way of "the Lord," now occurs in the form of particular characters, as John/Elijah preparing the way for Jesus.

This complicates the relationship between Jesus and God, anticipating what will soon become the Gospel's defining theological tension. For although the term "Lord" (κύριος) functions in Isa. 40:3 (quoted at Mark 1:3) and throughout the scriptural tradition as a reference to Yahweh, the God of Israel, Mark also seems to connect it to Jesus, the "Lord" whose way John/Elijah prepares.[6] This forces the audience into a more complex theological world—Jesus is no longer simply the anointed Son of God, as claimed by the Gospel's opening verse, but also the Lord himself. The narrative does not provide any means of resolving this tension but simply presents it. Whether John/Elijah prepares the way for God *or* Jesus is therefore not at issue, since Mark's answer to that question is a rather mysterious yes.[7] To the extent that Mark's opening allusions to Malachi continue to influence its experience of the subsequent narrative, the audience may also expect a connection between Jesus and God's end-time activity: "the great and terrible day of the Lord."

Only ten verses into the Gospel, then, the audience faces a distinct theological tension. Jesus is, on the one hand, the anointed Son whom God addresses via scriptural prophecy: "*I* am sending *my* messenger ahead of *you*, who will prepare *your* way." On the other hand, however, Jesus is the "Lord" whose way that same messenger prepares (1:3). The discourse distinguishes Jesus from God while also identifying them. This very tension Mark then encapsulates into a single scene—the baptism of Jesus by John/Elijah (1:10–11)—a scene that also introduces a major theological development: God's invasion of the world through Jesus. This event becomes the primary means by which Mark perpetuates the identification of God and Jesus, although certain details in the discourse also perpetuate the distinction between them.

JESUS ANOINTED/POSSESSED BY GOD

In many ways the simple act of being baptized reinforces a kind of distance between Jesus and God. One senses in the Synoptic redaction, for instance, an attempt to cover up the evident submission of Jesus to John/Elijah, however temporary it might be (1:4).[8] As if the preparation and arrival of God's "way" in the Judean countryside—far removed from the political-religious center of Jerusalem—were not surprising enough,[9] Mark depicts Jesus, the "Lord" of that same "way," as the passive recipient of an inferior's cleansing ritual. Despite the self-effacing prophecy of John/Elijah, then, Jesus submits to "a baptism of repentance for the forgiveness of sins" (1:4).

Is it true, then, that John/Elijah "fumbles the introduction"?[10] Has he simply failed to live up to his own prophecy? Given Mark's penchant for tension already evident in the narrative, this seems unlikely. Moreover, God responds to this very event, despite its potential scandal, by claiming Jesus as his own: "And a voice came from heaven, 'You are my Son, the Beloved; in you I am well pleased" (1:11). Spoken as Jesus emerges newly baptized from the Jordan River, this divine confirmation reinforces, through a partial quotation of Ps. 2:2, Jesus' royal status, forcing the audience to hold Jesus' submissive act in tension with his divine commission. Indeed, given that Psalm 2 is not merely a royal hymn but a coronation hymn, one can say that it is precisely through this temporary submission to John that Jesus is revealed to be the Christ (Anointed One) of God.

As with God's scriptural announcement at Mark 1:2–3, this direct speech reinforces God's own transcendence vis-à-vis Jesus: "You are my Son."[11] However, specific details in 1:10 suggest the beginning of God's invasive activity. Consider, first of all, that as Jesus rises up from his baptism he sees the heavens being "torn apart" (σχιζομένους), an implicit but powerful indication that

God's response to this anointing is much more than verbal. Unlike Matthew's and Luke's comparatively tame use of the verb ἀνοίγω ("open"),[12] the verb σχίζω denotes something more like an irreparable tear (what is opened can presumably be closed again). This jarring image seems to reflect a cosmology in which the heavens separate the powerful holiness of God from the world of mortals, much like the temple curtain protected priests from the divine presence within the Holy of Holies.[13] The barrier once separating God and humanity has therefore been taken away. True to form, God is making things happen.

Donald Juel entertains two possibilities for understanding the significance of this tearing. On the one hand, one might construe the elimination of the divine-human barrier, in the spirit of Heb. 10:19–22, as Mark's subtle exhortation to enter boldly into God's presence "by the new and living way that he opened for us" (Heb. 10:20). The tearing of the heavens means that humans now have "access" to God.[14] Juel, however, finds this parallel less suggestive than Isa. 64:1: "O that you would tear open the heavens and come down, so that the mountains would quake at your presence" (NRSV). If one follows this interpretive trajectory, the tearing of the heavens in Mark signals a divine initiative of rather unsettling proportions. The audience no longer hears a comforting invitation to enter confidently into God's presence but rather a potentially frightening announcement about "the removal of protection" that once shielded them from that presence.[15] Mark's point in this case is that God, "unwilling to be confined to sacred spaces, is on the loose in our own realm."[16] With respect to the larger plot, in which Jesus consistently mystifies and disturbs, this scriptural parallel seems considerably more Markan.

This interpretation also rings truer to the divine activity that immediately follows, for God does not rest with a torn heaven but continues, in a remarkable echo of Isa. 64:1, to "come down" (ירד). In Mark's words, Jesus sees "the Spirit descending (καταβαῖνον) like a dove into him" (1:10b). Equally significant, however, is the evident purpose of this descent—the Spirit descends "into" (εἰς) Jesus, so that his anointing is also a kind of possession. Here English versions unfortunately choose to translate the pronoun εἰς as "on" or "upon," a reading more indebted to the pronoun ἐπί as used by Matthew (3:16) and Luke (3:22).[17] Although this avoids some potential awkwardness in Mark's dove simile, it does so by suppressing the more fundamental theological point: this is no normal commissioning. Jesus does not merely receive God's Spirit like a crown "upon" his head but is rather possessed by that Spirit.[18] The same God who speaks to Jesus "from heaven" (1:11) is also the God who possesses him.[19]

This seems the best explanation for how that same Spirit can then "cast out" (ἐκβάλλω) Jesus into the wilderness for a period of testing (πειράζω) by Satan (1:12–13). God directs Jesus by virtue of his possession of him. The possession may even underlie why Jesus emerges from his testing unscathed (1:14–15).[20]

Yet it is still a period of *testing* that Jesus must endure with the aid of wild beasts and angels (1:13). In this way too the narrative interweaves two divergent dynamics with respect to God's relationship to Jesus.

Scholars bent on discerning a single meaning in the text may either miss this theological tension or dismiss it as the product of haphazard editorial activity (an editor compiling traditions without thought for narrative coherence). Even narrative critics, more likely to recognize the artistry of the Gospel, may struggle to account for such tension using traditional definitions of "characterization." As Philip Reubin Johnson notes, however, the "metaphysical awkwardness . . . needs to be understood as an element of characterization itself."[21] In other words, the tension itself says something about God. It should not be resolved, much less dismissed, but allowed to stand and contribute to one's understanding of God's role in the story.

JESUS PROCLAIMS GOD/HIMSELF

Mark's theologically charged introduction creates a distinctive narrative momentum with respect to the audience's experience of the ensuing plot. Expectations have been raised concerning God's role as main actor and, more specifically, the divergent modes of activity that make up that role. Turning now to the subsequent episode (1:14–15), one finds that Jesus' programmatic proclamation about "the reign of God" (βασιλεία τοῦ θεοῦ, 1:15) completes the audience's preparation for "the way of the Lord" while reinforcing its expectation for theological tension.[22]

"After John was arrested," Mark says, "Jesus came into Galilee preaching the good news of God [1:14] and saying, 'The time has been fulfilled, and the reign of God has drawn near. Repent and believe the good news' [1:15]." The parallel between verses 14 and 15 suggests that Jesus' speech in verse 15 elaborates upon the summary narration of verse 14. The "good news of God" is precisely that "the time has been fulfilled and the reign of God has drawn near." Jesus himself calls it "good news" that demands both repentance and faith. As with God's own speech about Jesus (1:2–3) and to Jesus (1:11), here Jesus' speech about God reinforces the distinction between them. Having been anointed by God, Jesus proclaims the nearing reign of God.

This dimension of the narrative discourse helps the audience tie together certain loose ends. For instance, the reappearance of the word "gospel," or "good news" (εὐαγγέλιον; twice in 1:14, 15), takes the audience back to 1:1: "the beginning of the gospel of Jesus Christ." Given this significant echo, the question arises as to how one understands the relationship between these two verses. In particular, how does one hear 1:1 in light of 1:14–15? Reading 1:1 as the Gospel's opening line, one naturally takes the phrase "gospel of Jesus Christ" to mean the gospel *about* Jesus Christ.[23] Given that Jesus functions as the main character of the entire narrative, this interpretation makes perfect sense: Mark's story, taken in its entirety, constitutes the good news about God's anointed Son.

Upon hearing 1:14–15, however, the audience no longer understands the "good news" strictly in connection with Jesus (1:1) but also in connection with God (1:14) and the nearness of God's reign (1:15). Thus a different interpretive possibility presents itself. For if Jesus is the narrative's main character, and if Jesus proclaims the "good news of God," then the "good news of Jesus Christ" (1:1) may also refer to the good news that Jesus proclaims.[24] The good news is not only Mark's story about Jesus but also Jesus' message about God. Thus Jesus functions as both the good news and the herald of good news.

In this way 1:14–15 exemplifies what Wolfgang Iser calls the "continual interplay between modified expectations and transformed memories" in the experience of narrative.[25] It shows how narrative creates a temporal and dynamic experience insofar as the meaning of Mark's opening line cannot be limited to a single narrative moment. On the question of Jesus' relationship to "the gospel," 1:1 generates expectations that are soon modified at 1:14–15, thereby also transforming the audience's memory of 1:1 (that is, how the audience understands its meaning). Stated simply, the relationship between Jesus and the gospel varies depending on the precise narrative moment one considers.

Interpreters bent on discerning a single Markan perspective will always be tempted to resolve any potential multivalence by pitting one interpretation against the other (what is "the" meaning of the text?).[26] A focus on the temporal and dynamic experience of Mark's story suggests, however, that one need not regard these two interpretive options as mutually exclusive. Rather, they represent two different places along the audience's narrative journey. Moreover, the argument in favor of upholding both interpretations may be further supported by what I have already said of Mark's theological discourse, which depicts God both transcendently and invasively vis-à-vis Jesus. Given these divergent modes of divine activity, one should not be altogether shocked to find that Jesus proclaims the good news about God (1:14–15) while also simultaneously being the good news (1:1). In this way the tension reflected in scholarly debates reflects the tension Mark himself creates in his depictions of Jesus, God, and the good news about them.

Thus one also need not limit Jesus' initial proclamation at 1:14–15 to a transcendent portrait of the Markan God. Rather, there is a sense in which Jesus "has the dubious and somewhat shameless honor of preaching himself."[27] That is, since God has possessed Jesus at his baptism, Jesus' announcement may be understood not so much as an announcement about a not-yet-present reign, but as an announcement about himself. God's reign has drawn near (ἤγγικεν) precisely because Jesus, the bearer of divine presence, has drawn near. At the same time, however, one cannot escape the distinction implied by Jesus' speech *about* God. God's transcendence vis-à-vis Jesus has not been lost, but neither has it been allowed to define, in singular fashion, the relationship between them. The narrative discourse attributes the encroaching reign to both an invasive and a transcendent God. To eliminate this tension is to rob the Gospel of both its narrative artistry and its theological significance.

CONCLUSION

To fully appreciate Mark's prologue one must take into account the way its discourse privileges the audience over the characters of the story (dramatic irony). In the introduction I mentioned how Mark depicts Jesus' baptism, or at least its immediate aftermath, as a kind of personal revelation. Even though large crowds (1:5) presumably witness the ritual itself, only Jesus seems to see the tearing heavens and the Spirit's descent (1:10), and only Jesus seems to hear God's confirmation from heaven (1:11).[28] That is, only Jesus *and* the audience see and hear these things. Likewise, when Jesus emerges from the wilderness proclaiming the nearness of God's reign, the audience alone is privy to the significance of his proclamation (though it is a significance defined by tension). One may very well imagine crowds, or at least passersby, standing within earshot. Yet there is no reason to believe that they would understand Jesus' words in the same way as the audience. Only the audience has heard Jesus in connection with God's ancient scriptural promises; only the audience has experienced the tension of God speaking to Jesus while simultaneously possessing him; and only the audience understands the multivalent good news about Jesus/God. Indeed, in his announcement of God's encroaching reign, there is a sense in which Jesus' primary audience is Mark's audience.[29]

In a story in which Jesus' identity and authority mystify other characters (8:29–33; 12:35–37; 15:31–32) and even factor into his own execution (14:61–64), it is difficult to underestimate the significance of this audience privileging. By virtue of the prologue, the audience is positioned to understand Jesus' subsequent teachings and deeds as demonstrations of his initial, paradigmatic proclamation. Indeed, by virtue of his possession by God, one could even say that everything Jesus says and does not only represents God's "nearing" reign but actually manifests it. God's reign is here and now, not in its eschatological entirety but rather in the form of what Brian Blount calls "a foreign pocket erupting into the territory of human present time."[30] Yet because Mark does not collapse the character of God into the character of Jesus, the audience can also expect God's continued transcendent activity. Hearers of the narrative cannot limit God, because the narrative itself refuses to do so. They have been prepared for a narrative journey filled with divine activity and theological tension.

In privileging its audience, however, the prologue does much more than transmit information; it also functions to draw the audience into the story itself. As James Hanson notes, Mark's discourse places hearers squarely within "the clash between expectations and reality,"[31] or, more specifically, between promises fulfilled and unfulfilled. So one finds, on the one hand, clear evidence of God's faithfulness in the narrative's scriptural beginning: John the Baptist appears as Elijah returned, preparing the "way of the Lord" (1:3) in anticipation of the "day of the LORD" (Mal. 4:5). Likewise Jesus emerges, with echoes of Psalm 2, as God's anointed Son and king. In tying the prologue so closely to Scripture, Mark suggests that the beginning of his narrative is but the continuation a much larger theological story. The Gospel begins in medias res, as God's fulfillment of ancient scriptural promises.

On the other hand, Mark never indicates that the outright consummation of God's eschatological reign has occurred. It "has come near" (perfect tense, ἤγγικεν, 1:15), but it has hardly arrived in the full sense of, for example, 13:26–27 (which even then foreshadows a time beyond the narrative). Indeed, the opening discourse gives clues that suggest a narrative ripe with conflict. The setting "in the wilderness" (1:3, 4, 12) recalls periods of both deliverance (the exodus from Egypt) and judgment/struggle (e.g., idolatry at Sinai, grueling journey) for God's people.[32] Nor does it bode well that Jesus emerges in public only "after John was arrested" (1:14), particularly since John prepares the way for Jesus (1:2–3, 7–8). Along these lines, God's reference to Jesus as the "beloved Son" (1:11) strikes an ominous tone, for the only scriptural precedent for the phrase occurs with the binding of Isaac (Gen. 22:2, 12, 16).[33]

Thus the prologue places hearers within a profound theological tension. They may take comfort, and place their hopes, in God's fulfillment of specific promises, but not without much uncertainty with regard to the story's future.[34] Moreover, that Mark introduces Jesus via the rite of baptism (as opposed to a manger or an eternal *logos*) reinforces the audience's vested interest in the outcome of this tension-filled narrative. For if Mark writes to fellow believers, as seems most likely, then the Gospel appropriately begins with their own beginning as Christians. The appropriateness of this beginning applies no less to the believing audience of the present day since, as Hanson notes, "John's preaching of baptism and Jesus' own summons to repent and believe link up with the defining experience of the 'Christian life.'"[35] Subsequent connections between Jesus' baptism and his death (10:38–40; 15:34–39) will later reveal a distinct direction to that life, so that hearers, having identified with Mark's baptismal introduction, will find themselves baptized into a world of conflict and hostility—just as God's Spirit propels Jesus from baptism to testing (1:12–13).

In all of these ways the Gospel prevents hearers from experiencing the story at "a safe distance."[36] Quite the opposite, it awakens the audience, whether ancient or contemporary, to its location between the beginning and the end, to a life lived in what Dan Via succinctly names "the middle of time."[37] Thus the audience travels along its narrative journey just as it travels through its own Christian pilgrimage, celebrating God's faithfulness while also anticipating future struggle. Indeed, to discover the full Markan perspective on that pilgrimage and God's role in it, the audience must continue along its narrative journey. Standing in the tension between beginning and end, it awaits the tension of a transcendent/invasive God.

2

God Calls/Fishes Disciples (Mark 1:16–20)

Happy exchange of fishing! Jesus fishes for them that they may become fishers of other fishermen.

—*Saint Jerome*[1]

And Jesus said to them, "Follow behind me, and I will make you become fishers of people." And immediately, leaving behind their nets, they followed him.

—*Mark 1:17–18*

Having heard Mark's prologue, the audience can no longer confine God to a scriptural memory. It moves along its narrative journey with expectations of divine activity, knowing the potential for God to act both transcendently and invasively vis-à-vis Jesus. At first glance such expectations may seem irrelevant to the subsequent scene in which Jesus calls his first disciples (Mark 1:16–20). For it is common, and in many ways quite appropriate, to understand the fishermen's collective response to Jesus as a strictly human decision, devoid of any divine influence. Based on the theological expectations generated by Mark's prologue, however, a rather different interpretive possibility emerges, one that does not replace the traditional view but stands alongside it. For if God has possessed Jesus at his baptism, then there is a sense in which God acts through Jesus to fish the fishermen (so to speak) into the eschatological kingdom drawn near. It is, as Saint Jerome notes, a "happy exchange of fishing." Viewed from this angle the scene represents God's first significant action toward characters other than Jesus, an action that also generates the audience's vested interest in the disciples and their future role in the story.

AMBIGUOUS FOLLOWING AND HUMAN VOLITION

The possibility for such divergent, yet equally valid, interpretations of the same scene stems from the narrative's sheer ambiguity regarding the disciples' motivation for following Jesus. Such motivation is in fact absent from the narrative altogether:

> And as [Jesus] was walking along the Sea of Galilee he saw Simon and his brother Andrew casting nets into the sea, for they were fishermen. And Jesus said to them, "Follow behind me, and I will make you become fishers of people." And immediately, leaving behind their nets, they followed him. And having gone a little further he saw James, the son of Zebedee, and his brother John in their boats mending nets. And immediately he called them, and they left their father Zebedee in the boat with the hired men, and they followed behind him (1:16–20).

Note that in both episodes (vv. 16–18, 19–20) Mark matter-of-factly describes only the call of Jesus and the following of the fishermen. Altogether absent is any form of verbal exchange (aside from Jesus' summons) that suggests the fishermen's motivation, much less any direct window into their collective state of mind. To bring even the most basic element of coherence to the narrative, hearers must therefore supply the explanation that the discourse omits. They must appeal to what Mark does not actually say.

Along these lines, the traditional interpretation of 1:16–20 is simple enough to treat only briefly. It operates out of the supposition (or, in some cases, presupposition) that all human action stems ultimately from human volition. Interpreters in this case take a seemingly universal rule with respect to human behavior and apply it to the narrative.[2] Thus, although the precise reasons may vary depending on the interpreter, the fishermen have in this view *willed* to follow Jesus. They have "chosen," "decided," "obeyed," "believed," and/or "repented." Among these possibilities not all prove equally convincing (see discussion below). Generally speaking, however, Mark's perfect ambiguity certainly allows for an interpretation based on human volition. One infers such an explanation even though Mark does not explicitly say, "the fishermen willed to follow Jesus."

This seems precisely the logic behind the redaction and expansion of Mark in Luke 5:1–12.[3] In this version of the story Jesus attracts his first disciples through a series of actions that elicit the required motivation. He teaches a crowd by the seaside (Luke 5:1–3), amazes it with a miraculous catch of fish (5:4–9), and only then summons the four fishermen, now convinced of his authority, to follow him (5:10). Thus one of Mark's earliest interpreters resolves the narrative's ambiguity by supplying a volition not explicitly stated in the narrative. This is not really an argument in favor of the traditional interpretation of the Markan account, for Luke says many things that Mark does not; and Mark's Gospel, at any rate, exercises its own narrative autonomy vis-à-vis its Synoptic redactors. The logic behind Luke's redaction, however, is essentially the same as the traditional approach to Mark 1:16–20. Some kind of volition must be inferred; otherwise the scene makes no sense.

Although he is not a biblical scholar, the literary theorist Seymour Chatman considers this approach a quite natural way of construing narrative:

> [O]ur minds inveterately seek structure, and they will provide it if necessary. Unless otherwise instructed, readers will tend to assume that even "The king died and the queen died" presents a causal link, that the king's death has something to do with the queen's. We do so in the same spirit in which we seek coherence in the visual field, that is, we are inherently disposed to turn raw sensation into perception. So one may argue that pure "chronicle" is difficult to achieve. "The king died and then the queen died" and "The king died and then the queen died of grief" differ narratively only in degrees of explicitness at the surface level; at the deeper structural level the causal element is present in both. The reader "understands" or supplies it; he infers that the king's death is the cause of the queen's. "Because" is inferred through ordinary presumptions about the world, including the purposive character of speech.[4]

Though rarely stated so openly, this is precisely the logic undergirding the traditional interpretation of Mark 1:16–20. Stated simply, Mark does not explicitly say, "the fishermen willed to follow Jesus," because he does not need to do so. Rather Mark expects, as it were, the audience naturally to supply the coherence for which the hurried narrative pace (particularly in his early chapters) does not always allow. One infers the volition of the fishermen "through ordinary presumptions about the world." Indeed, some justification for this explanation comes later in the narrative journey, when Jesus offers (qualified) praise for the disciples' radical commitment to him (10:28–31).

Yet it would be going too far, I think, to say that the narrative discourse allows only this interpretation. Nor is the search for alternative interpretations a purely modern, or postmodern, tendency. Writing some sixteen hundred years ago, Jerome (347–420 CE) makes the following observation about the same passage: "Unless there was something divine in the face of the Savior, [the fishermen] acted without reason in following a man whom they had never seen. Does one dismiss a father and follow a man in whom he sees nothing more than his father? . . . Why does [the Evangelist] say all of this? There was something divine showing itself in the face of the Savior that men, seeing, followed."[5]

Given that this is Jesus' first encounter with those who will soon be his disciples, Jerome rightly recognizes the oddity of the fishermen's "immediate" response to Jesus' summons.[6] Indeed, one does not normally "dismiss a father and follow a man in whom he sees nothing more than his father." In his own way, then, Jerome realizes that Mark's ironic privileging of the audience comes at the expense of the characters in the story. The fishermen have no recourse to Mark's prologue. They have not heard Jesus identified as God's anointed Son (1:1, 11); they have not seen God's Spirit descend into him (1:10); and they have not heard his announcement about God's encroaching kingdom (1:14–15).

That is why, among the different versions of the traditional interpretation, a motivation grounded either in repentance or outright recognition (of Jesus' true identity) is most unlikely.[7] The fishermen do not respond to Jesus' kingdom proclamation (1:15), much less to any preceding scriptural announcement, but rather to one of the most enigmatic statements in the entire Gospel: "Follow behind me, and I will make you become fishers of people" (1:17).[8] To be sure, the *audience* has every reason to understand Jesus' summons in relation to his messianic identity and kingdom proclamation (see discussion below). Indeed, there is a sense in which the call to follow speaks directly to the Gospel's hearers who must, according to Whitney Shiner, "project" their own faith into the narrative.[9] To the extent that the fishermen (as opposed to the audience) follow by their own volition, however, that volition seems to originate in, and respond to, the invitation to fish for people.

That is also why Jerome's final interpretation, in my view, amounts more to speculation than interpretation, for it altogether dismisses Jesus' invitation in favor of an unspoken radiance in Jesus' face. The call to fish for people is no longer merely enigmatic but now, evidently, impossible as an effective invitation. The logic of Mark's discourse does not challenge Jerome's interpretive imagination; instead it drives him to imagine a completely different scenario whereby the fishermen are essentially attracted to Jesus quite apart from Jesus' own invitation. Rather than dismissing their response as impossible, however, I think it more appropriate to accept the scenario Mark has depicted and explore the possibility for human volition within those parameters. While I do not wish to delineate a precise motivation beyond this (blind faith? curiosity? ambition?), I think it necessary to recognize the logic of Mark's discourse on this point.

Despite the inadequacies of Jerome's final interpretation, he is certainly right to note the strange ambiguity of 1:16–20. Indeed, he recognizes what many modern interpreters do not, namely, that one cannot make sense of the scene without appealing to what Mark does not explicitly say.[10] Moreover, I appreciate Jerome's attempt to resolve the ambiguity theologically, by appeal to a kind of divine redirecting that "changed the direction of those who gazed upon [Jesus]" ("ad se contuentium oculos facile conuertebant").[11] In the following discussion I will forward an interpretation that retains this sense of redirecting. Yet instead of attributing it to a kind of divinity (*diuinus*) in Jesus' face, I will attribute it to the irresistible authority that Jesus' summons carries by virtue of his possession by God's Spirit. One can make sense of the ambiguity, in other words, by appealing to expectations generated by the prologue, particularly Mark's depiction of God as the story's main actor. Thus Jesus' summons functions not merely as an invitation to Mark's audience (à la Shiner) but as a profound statement about Jesus' divinely empowered speech.

THE CASE FOR DIVINE FISHING

Even before Jesus takes center stage, one finds a hint of divine "attraction" in Mark's depiction of John's ministry. For it is surely no coincidence that the scriptural anticipation of God's renewed activity (1:2–3) gives rise to an enormous exodus of people into the wilderness: "And the whole (πᾶσα) Judean countryside and all (πάντες) the people of Jerusalem were going out to him" (1:5). Here Mark's hyperbole, though perhaps on the surface a mere exaggeration, plays a crucial theological role. With God's renewed activity announced by Scripture, 1:5 illustrates the extent to which God's impending presence alters the world, attracting even those not fully aware of what will soon happen. As God prepares to invade the world, people flock to God's messenger in inconceivable numbers, moving from the center of religious governance (Jerusalem) to the peripheral beginning of "the way of the Lord" (1:3). One may even understand such movement as part of God's preparations.

The specific location of God's way "in the wilderness" (ἐν τῇ ἐρήμῳ, 1:3–4, 12–13) also brings to mind what is arguably the most formative event in the history of Israel: the exodus out of Egypt.[12] Joel Marcus goes so far as to suggest that, in addition to the physical setting, Mark's use of the verb ἐκπορεύομαι (1:5) echoes Israel's original "coming out" of bondage.[13] At the very least, one may safely say that Mark's Scriptures remember Israel's time in the wilderness, as well as the events surrounding that time, as an era of unwavering divine involvement. God hears the cries of the Israelites in bondage (Exod. 3:7); God delivers the Israelites from that bondage (Exod. 12:1–15:21); God provides for the Israelites in the wilderness (Exod. 15:21–17:16); God institutes commandments and laws in the wilderness (Exod. 20–24); and, finally, God "tabernacles" among the Israelites in the wilderness (Exod. 35–40). To be sure, Israel's first wilderness sojourn produces some of its most intensely theological memories.

Of particular interest for interpreters of Mark 1:5 is the specific manner in which Israel comes to remember this theological experience. For a major strand of biblical tradition formulates its memory of the exodus in terms of God as an acting subject, with Israel as a passive object. Consequently, Israel's Scriptures repeatedly recall the exodus as a divine act by which God, quite literally, "brought out" (ἐξάγω) or "brought up" (ἀνάγω) Israel from Egypt into the wilderness.[14] Though recalled almost exclusively in the context of Israel's contrasting rebellion,[15] these passages underscore, precisely through such a contrast, God's faithfulness to Israel from its very inception. Perhaps the best example of this theological pattern comes in Ps. 77:51–55 LXX:

> And [God] struck down (ἐπάταξεν) all the firstborn in Egypt,
> the first of their many hardships in the tents of Ham.
> And as a shepherd he took up (ἀπῆρεν) his people
> and he brought them up (ἀνήγαγεν), as a flock, in the wilderness
>   (ἐν ἐρήμῳ)
> and he guided (ὡδήγησεν) them in hope, and they were not afraid,
> and the sea covered their enemies.
> And he led them to (εἰσήγαγεν) the mountain of his sanctuary,
> [the mountain] which his right hand acquired.
> And he cast out (ἐξέβαλεν) the nations from before them
> and he distributed the land (ἐκληροδότησεν) to them as a line of
>   inheritance
> and the tribes of Israel he made to dwell (κατεσκήνωσεν) in their tents.

Here Israel's grammar bespeaks its theology: God, as the subject of a series of third-person verbs, acts upon Israel (as well as its enemies). The grammar asserts an element of divine activity that, while perhaps less explicit in the book of Exodus, becomes a dominant motif in Israel's subsequent interpretations of those events. Stated simply, Israel remembers God as the main actor of its story: God takes up the people; God brings out the people; God guides the people; God leads the people; and God plants the people.

This is not to suggest that Mark actually wrote the prologue to his Gospel with Psalm 77 in mind. The precise scriptural echoes that Mark "intended" to invoke (if he intended any at all) lie well beyond the limits of academic inquiry.[16] Nevertheless, Mark's Scriptures do provide a distinctive theological pattern that, when placed alongside Mark 1:5, suggests that God functions as the primary actor who, in the spirit of Psalm 77, moves corporate Israel into the wilderness. Such an interpretation makes good sense in light of the preceding announcement of God's preparations "in the wilderness" (Mark 1:3) as well as the following account of God's invasion of the world through Jesus (1:9–11). Although clearly hyperbolic, then, 1:5 is no mere hyperbole. Nor does it suggest only a mass exodus into the wilderness. Much more than that, it suggests, precisely through its hyperbole, God's own activity in the story. It stands to reason, then, that although Jesus will soon openly proclaim "the gospel of God" (1:14), there is a sense in which that same gospel has begun "before it is proclaimed to have begun."[17]

Taken alongside God's subsequent tearing of the heavens and possession of Jesus (1:10), God's attracting of the Judean masses constitutes a significant theological precedent with which the audience may resolve the ambiguity of 1:17–20.[18] For if God can announce his own activity via Scripture, draw masses of people to the Jordan River, and invade the world via the Son, then it stands to reason that God can also attract a few random fishermen. In this way one finds confirmation, along the Sea of Galilee, of expectations generated in the wilderness: God functions as the story's main actor and therefore fishes, so to speak, the fishermen. Over the course of a long and meandering narrative path, Simon, Andrew, James, and John represent God's first real "catch."

Perhaps not by coincidence, the very next scene (1:21–28) exhibits the same potential for God to act upon characters through Jesus. Moving into a Capernaum synagogue (2:21), Jesus encounters a man who, speaking with the voice of the spirit possessing him, identifies Jesus as "the Holy One of God" (1:24). In response, Jesus commands the spirit to silence, casting it out with an immediacy reminiscent of 1:17–20; for no sooner has Jesus exclaimed, "Come out of him!" (1:25) than Mark tells the audience, "It came out of him" (1:26). It is difficult to miss the parallel to the previous scene, in which Jesus' summons creates an "immediate" (1:18) response from the fishermen. The dynamic in the Capernaum synagogue confirms what the prologue only anticipates: God can, through his possession of Jesus, exercise a kind of irresistible influence over characters in the narrative. Bearing God's presence, Jesus does not always conform to the expectations of (limited) human power. Thus the crowd of onlookers, privy to the exorcism but not to the demon's identification of Jesus, exclaims with bewildered wonder: "What is this? A new teaching with authority! He commands even the unclean spirits, and they obey him!" (1:27). This supposedly new and mysterious "authority" (ἐξουσία) the audience easily attributes to God.[19] No wonder, then, that the unclean spirit offers no resistance.

Only a highly distracted audience would miss the repetition of this dynamic in subsequent passages. For instance, the call of Levi employs an ambiguous call-and-response pattern identical to that of 1:20: "He said to him, 'Follow me.' And getting up, he followed him" (2:14). Jesus' miracles, furthermore, tend to follow the example of his first exorcism at 2:21–28. He cleanses a leper (1:41–42), heals a paralytic (2:11–12), raises a synagogue leader's daughter (5:41–42), and restores a blind man's sight (10:52), all by the "immediate" (εὐθύς) power of his words. Even when lacking the common term "immediately," Mark's narration suggests the same instant and authoritative efficacy, as when Jesus stills the storm on the Sea of Galilee: "He said to the sea, 'Be quiet!' It was silenced" (4:39).[20] Such a pervasive accent on Jesus' powerful speech lends considerable weight to the insight of Jerome, who writes that the fishermen follow Jesus because "the very speech of the Lord was creative; likewise, whatever he spoke brought about its work."[21]

UPHOLDING AND GAUGING THE TENSION

Before exploring the full implications for this interpretation, it is worth repeating the opening tone of this chapter: Mark's ambiguity invites *tension*. In so emphasizing the way Jesus "fishes" the fishermen, one risks obscuring this tension. Yet I do not mean to dismiss the possibility—even the actuality—of the fishermen following Jesus out of their own volition. Rather I mean to complement that interpretation with an equally valid one. In complementing the traditional interpretation, however, I am also complicating the rather simplistic, and largely unspoken, assumption that a single text "contains" only a single meaning. For if the ambiguity of 1:16–20 allows for two sharply divergent explanations, then Mark's interpreters should uphold that tension instead of resolving or alleviating it. Much like the prologue, such tension proves an important moment along the audience's narrative journey.

Most of the scholarly literature does not uphold the tension of 1:16–20 because it rarely bothers to explore interpretations outside the traditional one. Yet one does find the tension incipient, so to speak, in the work of a handful of scholars—even though they do not acknowledge the tension as such. For instance, Lamar Williamson notes the way in which Jesus "acts . . . as the fisherman" on the one hand, while also crediting the fishermen with "obedience" on the other hand (thus making the disciples, one presumes, obliging fish).[22] In a similar vein, Hugh Anderson speaks of the "sovereignty" of Jesus' summons while also insisting that the fishermen "must say Yes or No" in response to it.[23] Finally, Eduard Schweizer states in his 1970 commentary that the fishermen "are *made* disciples by the call of Jesus, which is as powerful as the *creative word* of God (Ps 33:9; Isa 55:10f.)."[24] Yet in a later essay he claims the fishermen "had to let this happen."[25]

In all of these examples one sees a tension between the power of Jesus' summons and the volition of the fishermen. It is precisely the kind of tension I have tried to highlight: God fishes the fishermen via Jesus *and* the fishermen "will to follow" Jesus. Yet these interpreters show no awareness of having touched upon two divergent explanations for the same passage. They either emphasize the power of Jesus' summons only to qualify it (as with Williamson and Anderson) or they assert them both as if they logically cohere (as with Schweizer, albeit in two separate works). In every case, however, the quest for a single meaning seems to preclude the acknowledgment, or even possibility, of tension within the narrative. Thus the few scholars who touch upon

Jesus' powerful summons eventually return to the safer confines of the traditional interpretation.

Perhaps the only exception to this rule is Joel Marcus, whose recent work breaks entirely from the traditional view. Marcus begins by noting the parallel between Jesus' "calling" (καλέω) of disciples and God's own "calling" of prophets in the Old Testament, concluding from this parallel that "the call of God undergirds the call of Jesus."[26] Yet it is not merely a matter of Jesus speaking on God's behalf. Rather, for Marcus, the lack of reference to the fishermen's motivation points to "the overwhelming power of Jesus' word; all human reticence has been instantaneously washed away because *God* has arrived on the scene in the person of Jesus, and it is *his* compelling voice that speaks through Jesus' summons."[27] Here one finds neither qualification nor confusion but an unequivocal assertion of Jesus' divine power over the entirely passive fishermen. Marcus recognizes how God's "compelling voice"—what I have called God's fishing—does not logically cohere with the traditional interpretation. For if God really fishes the fishermen, then the fishermen do not choose to follow. After all, fish do not obey but are caught.

Yet despite his radical departure from the traditional interpretation, Marcus continues to share a fundamental presupposition with its advocates, namely, that the text can have only one meaning. While most preclude, or seriously qualify, God's action in the story on the basis of the fishermen's volition, Marcus precludes the fisherman's volition on the basis of God's action. In both cases, however, one understands Mark's ambiguity as a problem to be resolved in entirely univocal terms. Such an either/or approach stems naturally from the aforementioned spatialization of the text into a container of single meaning (thus Chatman's above reference to the text's "deep structure"). However, in conceiving of Mark's Gospel as a hearing experience—and thus a kind of meandering journey—one opens the door to a both/and approach to the same narrative. Hence Mark's ambiguity ceases to be a problem and becomes simply a moment of dual possibility, even dual meaning. Because the possibilities do not logically cohere, it is also a moment of tension. The disciples will, and do not will, to follow. God invites the fishermen, and God fishes the fishermen.

How does one gauge this tension of 1:17 against the tension of the prologue? As I have already noted, an appeal to God's fishing activity stems from, and confirms, expectations generated in the prologue regarding God's role as main actor. More specifically, such an appeal draws on the potential for God to act invasively vis-à-vis Jesus, for it is precisely by virtue of God's possession of Jesus that Jesus bears God's presence and speaks God's powerful word. One might also say that God's transcendent activity comes to bear on this scene, though in an indirect sense, to the degree that God's transcendent activity in the prologue helped to generate expectations of divine activity. In explaining exactly why the disciples follow Jesus, however, one's appeal to God's fishing activity is essentially an appeal to God's invasive, rather than transcendent, action. Meanwhile the traditional interpretation draws strictly upon the audience's "ordinary presumptions about the world" (human action stems from human volition) and does not generally recognize the potential for divine activity at all. This does not mean that it is "wrong," of course, but only that it rules out God's action in this particular, and very brief, scene.

Thus the tension of 1:1–15 is not strictly identical to the tension of 1:16–20. While the former passage creates a tension between two divergent modes of divine activity, the latter creates a tension between human activity and (a specific mode of) divine activity. Indeed, it is precisely by acknowledging and expecting the first tension that one comes to experience the second. For without a prior openness to God's potential action in the narrative, an audience can only explain the developing plot in strictly human terms. Once God enters the equation, however, alternative explanations become possible, explanations that have the potential to create tension. Such is the case with 1:16–20.

THE ESCHATOLOGICAL SIGNIFICANCE OF FISHING

To this point I have described the tension surrounding why the fishermen initially follow Jesus. There remains, however, the question of what purpose, from Jesus' perspective, such following seeks to fulfill. While the first question wrestles with the ambiguity of Mark's narrative (the absence of any stated explanation), the second deals with Jesus' enigmatic words: "I will make you become fishers of people" (ποιήσω ὑμᾶς γενέσθαι ἁλιεῖς ἀνθρώπων, 1:17). Here I hope to shed light on the eschatological significance of this statement by reading it, in the context of Jesus' initial kingdom proclamation (1:15), as a promise of participation in God's shalom-making invasion of the world.

As previously stated, I do not mean to imply that the disciples actually hear Jesus' proclamation of God's reign, for 1:14–15 and 1:16–20 represent two distinct scenes. With respect to Mark's narrative discourse, however, the audience hears all of 1:14–20 in sequence, so that the first scene influences its experience of the second in a decidedly theological way. Thus, while Jesus' proclamation of God's reign does not constitute the precise invitation to which the fishermen respond, it does provide an eschatological backdrop against which the audience understands the purpose of Jesus' ministry and therefore the purpose of the disciples' following. What Simon, Andrew, James, and John see only as a stranger walking along the lakeside, the audience recognizes as both herald and agent of God's encroaching reign. To follow this herald/agent, then, is presumably to enter into some kind of relationship with that same reign.

Also worth recalling is my argument from the previous chapter regarding the multivalent character of Jesus' proclamation at 1:14–15. To the extent that God acts invasively vis-à-vis Jesus, one hears this proclamation as an announcement of that very invasion—God's eschatological reign encroaching into the present time. Yet to the extent that God acts transcendently vis-à-vis Jesus, one hears it more as a drawing near—God's eschatological reign approaching the present time. Thus Mark maintains a paradoxical balance between present and future, with both trajectories meeting in the person of Jesus. Following Blount, then, one can say on the one hand that in the "various manifestations of [Jesus'] preaching, e.g., the healings, the exorcisms, and the teachings, God's future power invade[s] and transform[s] the human present."[28] This is what it means to speak of Jesus as agent, and not merely herald, of God's reign. On the other hand, however, Jesus can continue to speak of that reign as a not-yet-completed reality, as a reign that faces obstacles (4:1–20) and awaits full consummation beyond the end of the narrative (13:26; 14:62).

Keeping in mind Jesus' eschatological proclamation, it is surely no coincidence that Jesus summons his first disciples with an equally eschatological promise. For it has long been acknowledged that scriptural precedents for the phrase "fishers of people" (ἁλιεῖς ἀνθρώπων, 1:17), though failing to match Mark's precise wording, speak unanimously of God's future judgment upon the "fish" to be caught.[29] Among these passages, the victims of God's metaphorical fishing/hunting are caught by means of either hook/snare (2 Kgs. 19:28; Job 19:6; Isa. 24:17; 37:29; Ezek. 29:4; 38:4; Amos 4:2; Hab. 1:14–17) or net (Jer. 16:16; Lam. 1:13; Ezek. 12:13; 17:20; 19:8; 32:3; Hos. 7:12; Hab. 1:14–17). Furthermore, they represent both Israelites (Job 19:6; Jer. 16:16; Lam. 1:13; Ezek. 12:13; 17:20; 19:8; Hos. 7:12; Amos 4:2; Hab. 1:14–17) and non-Israelites (2 Kgs. 19:28; Isa. 24:17; 37:29; Ezek. 29:4; 32:3; 38:4).[30] Despite these differences in detail, however, the fishing/hunting metaphor consistently refers to future judgment.[31] God's fishers enact God's will in a world that has neglected that will.

Particularly noteworthy is Jeremiah's description of Judah's imminent exile at the hands of the Babylonians (Jer. 16:16–17 LXX), a divine judgment brought about by Judah's idolatry (Jer. 16:11, 18): "Behold, I am sending out many fishers (ἁλεεῖς), says the Lord, and they will fish (ἁλιεύσουσιν) them, and after these things I will send out many hunters, and they will hunt them, over every mountain, and over every hill, and out of the holes of the rocks. Because my eyes are upon all of their ways, and their wrongdoings were not hidden from before my eyes." For the purposes of understanding Mark 1:17, Jeremiah's prophecy offers two suggestive parallels. First, of those passages that speak of God's metaphorical fishing/hunting, only Jeremiah 16, like Mark 1:16–17, uses the noun ἁλιεύς ("fisherman"). Second, Jeremiah's description of the fishermen as divine agents

("I am sending out fishers") closely resembles the Markan narrative, in which Jesus represents God's invasive action in the world. Based on these scriptural parallels, then, one can at least say that the disciples, as "fishers of people," will act, much like their new leader, as agents of God's eschatological reign. Regardless of whether the fishermen themselves recognize this new vocation (if so, it is a possible motivation for following), Mark's discourse makes such a promise to the audience.

Of course the parallels to Scripture are not perfect. For the disciples will soon discover what Mark's audience likely already knows, that their role as God's fishermen lacks the violence inherent in the scriptural tradition. The disciples will not annihilate God's enemies; rather, far from inflicting violence, the disciples will fall victim to it (8:34; 10:30; 13:9). Mark has therefore modified a scriptural metaphor to fit his own narrative purposes. As fishers of people, the disciples will bring God's transformative reign in a distinctively christological form. They will announce and enact divine judgment just as Jesus does—through proclamation (3:14; 6:12; 13:10), exorcisms (3:15; 6:7, 13), and outreach (6:37–44; 8:1–10). And, like their leader, they will meet the fate of God's judgment-speaking prophets, standing trial before councils and synagogues for their actions (13:9–11).

This explanation differs noticeably from the traditional interpretation of 1:17, according to which the phrase "fishers of people" denotes a specifically missionary activity, namely, the gathering of people into the church community. This view is articulated well by Jack Dean Kingsbury:

> The purpose of discipleship is announced by Jesus in his call to Simon and Andrew: "Come after me, and I shall make you become fishers of men" (1:17). Plainly, discipleship has "mission work" as its purpose. Striking is the universal nature of the mission Jesus envisages. At this juncture in Mark's story, Jesus is just beginning his ministry to Israel. Already, however, his vision encompasses not only the pre-Easter mission of the disciples to Israel (6:7–13) but also their post-Easter mission to the nations (13:10; 14:9).[32]

Of course, Mark's Gospel makes an inseparable connection between discipleship on the one hand, and the "universal nature" of the gospel on the other hand. In this sense Kingsbury rightly notes the significance of Jesus' prophecy about the disciples' future mission: "The gospel must first be proclaimed to all nations" (13:10), that is, to all the peoples outside Israel. Such proclamation certainly implies a future ingathering of believers. The real question, however, is whether Jesus' *initial summons* to the first disciples—"I will make you become fishers of people" (1:17)—reflects this same concern, particularly since all scriptural precedents reflect such a rather different one. Is it really necessary to contrast the Markan and scriptural usages, as some commentators do, as if one were "positive" and the other "negative"?[33]

The long-standing reticence to acknowledge a stronger parallel stems largely from the consistent use of the fishing metaphor in Scripture to denote a markedly violent judgment. As I have argued, however, one need not denote such violence in order to find a parallel. For if Mark has modified the metaphor to suit his story of Jesus, then he has essentially invited his audience to understand God's transformative, eschatological reign differently. But it is still a point about God's reign, namely, that it will come, at least incipiently, via human agents, albeit agents modeled on a crucified Messiah. Contrary to the traditional view, this eschatological subtext to 1:17 fits quite well with the opening of the Gospel, in which Mark describes the encroachment of God's reign into the present world. More to the point, it suggests that when Jesus promises to make "fishers of people" he anticipates a time when his disciples will extend this divine invasion—or, perhaps more appropriately, when God will extend it through the disciples.

In this way the disciples' task as God's fishermen resembles that of their leader, who promises it to them by virtue of his own divine authority. As Robert Tannehill notes, there is a sense in which "Jesus fulfills his commission by sharing it with others."[34] Thus it is surely not coincidental but rather theologically significant that in the narrative's two primary commissioning scenes (3:13–15; 6:6b–13) the audience hears language identical to previous descriptions of Jesus' own ministry.[35] This connection leads Blount to comment that the disciples also represent "the transformative power of the future kingdom in the present human circumstance."[36] Like Jesus, then, they bring wholeness to a broken world by exorcising demons (6:13), feeding the hungry (6:27; 8:6), and, within the context of these activities, proclaiming the message of God's reign (3:14; 6:11; 13:9). Taken together, these activities constitute the disciples' vocation as "fishers of people."

Compared to the traditional interpretation, this explanation of 1:17 better accounts for both its scriptural precedents and the subsequent descriptions of the disciples' activity within the narrative. Yet this is not to dismiss the traditional interpretation, since Mark's references to the disciples' proclamation do imply an eventual ingathering of new believers. It would simply be more accurate to say that such ingathering represents only a single dimension of a grand, eschatological vocation. Or, perhaps even more accurately, it is a natural consequence of that vocation—just as Jesus compels certain individuals to faith based on his powerful, shalom-making ministry (2:5; 5:34, 36; 9:23–24; 10:52). In the end, then, the traditional interpretation is not wrong but simply inadequate by itself, particularly with respect to God's invasive activity and the disciples' promised role as human agents of that activity.

CONCLUSION

At two different levels Mark 1:16–20 reinforces expectations created by Mark's prologue. At the most general level it reinforces expectations of tension. While the tension here is not identical with that of the prologue, it is clearly a tension related to God. Along these lines, 1:16–20 also reinforces expectations regarding God's decisive action in the narrative, particularly God's invasive action via the ministry of Jesus (God's transcendent activity will be reinforced later in the narrative). Although this is not the only explanation for the fishermen's immediate response to Jesus, it is certainly a viable one grounded in Mark's theological discourse.

Hence it is also an explanation that generates new expectations. For the scenario I have described makes clear to the audience that God's action in the narrative is not confined to the person of Jesus but can, potentially at least, bear directly upon the actions of those whom Jesus encounters. The question therefore arises as to what form these subsequent encounters might take. As the audience will soon discover, Jesus' divine authority finds a home among those whom it helps, while it elicits hostility from those whose own authority it threatens. Indeed, the power of the latter group will ultimately prevail over the former, leading to the ultimate isolation of Jesus in his final hours (15:11).

Perhaps the most important development in 1:16–20 is the introduction of a new character group, followers of Jesus commissioned to extend God's transformative, eschatological reign into the world. Yet the scene "is not complete in itself but is the beginning of a story line,"[37] for the promise to become God's fishers is asserted without being realized. Thus the audience now holds expectations for the disciples just as it does for God and Jesus. However, it is precisely because the disciples' future vocation is *promised* that the audience's expectations for the disciples overlap with its expectations for Jesus and especially for God. Put simply, the disciples cannot make themselves God's fishers. "I will make you," Jesus says. This "making," the narrative implies, is not simply a matter of Jesus' power but—to be more precise—of God's power working through Jesus. For it is God, after all, who has commissioned and possessed Jesus in the first place. In this way 1:17 brings the question of God's faithfulness to bear directly upon the fate of the disciples.

Nor is the question of God's faithfulness something the audience can entertain disinterestedly, at a "safe distance" from the Gospel's unfolding plot. Rather it is precisely the issue of God's faithfulness that draws the audience even deeper into the narrative. This is particularly the case if one imagines a believing audience, in which hearers consider themselves followers of Jesus and the God he represents. As Hanson notes, "the intense investment in the disciples on the part of Jesus (and God) has intertwined their fate with the fate of the promise of the gospel, making the question of their fate a matter of utmost—and existential—concern for the audience."[38] The disciples are supposed to play an integral role in the unfolding story of God. Thus 1:16–20 effectively ensures the audience's vested interest (not just its casual interest) in the disciples, even as the subsequent narrative challenges its assumptions about how and when they will conform to Jesus' expectations.

In this way 1:16–20 draws the audience deeper into the tension of promises fulfilled and endangered, by extending that tension to the future of the disciples. As noted in chapter one, the prologue first generates this tension by depicting God's renewed activity (in the fulfillment of Scripture) on the one hand, while foreshadowing obstacles to God's full reign on the other hand. So also in the gathering of Jesus' first disciples, the audience hears confirmation of Jesus' divine authority in the simple alignment of the fishermen "after" (ὀπίσω) Jesus (1:17); yet that very alignment also suggests, in its ominous echo of John the Baptist's preaching (1:7), the potential for conflict as well. For the audience will recall that Jesus came "after" John and that John's divinely coordinated ministry ended in arrest.[39] Once again, the audience may take comfort in certain events, but not without facing uncertainty, if not also dread, with regard to the story's future.

This tension surrounding the disciples' fate reaches a disturbing climax when the audience completes its narrative journey only to find the promise of 1:17 endangered: Jesus' followers abandon him to the cross and, perhaps even more disturbingly, fail to report the news of his resurrection. In this way the Gospel not only begins but also ends in "the middle of time,"[40] challenging the audience to consider if any progress (for lack of a better word) has even been achieved along the way. Thus when hearers, standing at the end of their narrative journey, look back upon Jesus' call of the fishermen, they are forced to "imagine there is something promising simply in his choice."[41] They must trust Jesus' promise even beyond the end of the narrative, hoping that the God of Jesus will ultimately prove faithful.

3

God Confounds/Hardens Disciples (Mark 1:21–8:21)

[B]eing an insider is only a more elaborate way of being kept outside.
—*Frank Kermode*[1]

Do you have hearts that have been hardened?
—*Mark 8:17–18*

For all of the ambiguity and tension of Mark 1:16–20, one clear promise reverberates: "I will make you become fishers of people" (1:17). As a result of this promise, those whom the audience initially views as ordinary fishermen it now views as disciples set aside for a special task. They will, according to Jesus, spread God's transformative reign into a presently broken world.

As I noted at the end of chapter two, however, the Gospel creates a significant theological dilemma by not depicting the full realization of this promise. Between Mark's fourth and tenth chapters, for instance, the disciples manage to misunderstand, to varying degrees, virtually everything about Jesus: the nature of his own ministry (8:27–9:1; 9:30–37; 10:32–45), his parables (4:13; 7:17), his power over nature (4:41; 6:35, 49–50, 52; 8:4, 17), his transfiguration (9:5–6), his casting out of a specific kind of spirit (9:18, 28), and the nature of his healing power (5:31). In addition to this misunderstanding—if not also related to it—Mark depicts the disciples' wholesale abandonment of Jesus (14:27, 50; 15:66–72), concluding his Gospel with the scandal of women disciples fleeing the empty tomb in disobedient silence. At the end of the narrative, then, the disciples seem anything but "fishers of people." Indeed, the momentum of the Gospel's ending seems to move in the opposite direction.

Scholars generally attribute these failures to a kind of ineptitude, for which the audience must hold the disciples themselves accountable.[2] More specifically,

I contend that the disciples fail to recognize Jesus' role as agent of God's eschatological reign. Ironically, it is the very manifestation of that reign, through the powerful deeds of Jesus, that confounds the disciples, creating responses parallel to the witnesses of Jesus' first exorcism in Capernaum: "What is this? A new teaching with authority!" (1:27; see 4:41). No wonder, then, that Jesus makes repeated attempts to correct their misguided responses (4:13–20, 33, 40; 6:37–44, 50–51). Indeed, it is precisely Jesus' exasperation that encourages the audience to frown upon the disciples' ineptitude.

At the same time, however, I do not believe this explanation alone suffices, for it does not account for certain crucial elements of Mark's discourse. It does account for how God's invasive mode of action confounds the disciples. But it overlooks references to God's transcendent mode of action, particularly a series of allusions to God's own hardening of the disciples (4:13; 6:52; 8:17–18). Though few in number (and thus largely ignored by scholars), these references suggest that the disciples' struggles, which elicit Jesus' own amazement (4:13; 8:17–18), are less a matter of ineptitude than of divine concealment. With respect to God's transcendent action, then, the audience comes to see the truth in Frank Kermode's claim that "being an insider is only a more elaborate way of being kept outside"[3]—at least within the confines of Mark's narrative (cf. 13:9–13).[4]

In this way the tension surrounding Mark's depiction of the disciples stems directly from the tension already inherent in his depiction of God. In other words, the audience cannot isolate a single explanation for the disciples' misunderstanding because it cannot isolate a single explanation for God's action in the narrative. It must rather hold together two logically opposite scenarios. Precisely for this reason, Mark's depiction of the disciples is simpler, and considerably more profound, than a "problem" to be solved by interpreters. It is rather an experience of God's mystery.

Continuing to honor the Gospel as a temporal and dynamic experience, I will examine this mystery as it unfolds along the audience's meandering narrative journey. This approach will bring to light how Mark's depiction of the disciples defies expectations generated in the Gospel's early chapters (1:21–4:12), in which the disciples quickly conform—or seem to conform—to the promise of 1:17. No sooner does such conformity appear certain than Mark begins to reveal the disciples' troubling tendency toward misunderstanding (4:13, 40; 6:45–52; 8:14–21), simultaneously dropping clues to God's hardening activity (6:52; 8:17–18). This development complicates the audience's perception of the disciples as "insiders" firmly aligned with Jesus. It does not thwart that perception, however, because Mark interweaves his references to misunderstanding and hardening with brief windows into the disciples' successful work as God's fishers (6:7–13, 30–44; 8:1–10, 14–21).

CLOSE ALIGNMENT WITH JESUS (1:21–4:34)

Disciples as Family of Jesus (1:21–3:35)

Beginning with the initial call of the fishermen, Mark gives the audience every indication that the disciples form a privileged group in relation to Jesus. Consequently, this early characterization reinforces the audience's preliminary expectations for the disciples by moving them closer, it seems, to the realization of Jesus' promise at 1:17.

How does Mark create this impression? To begin, the simple act of following—whether as a result of human volition or divine fishing—illustrates the disciples' close alignment with their leader. Yet other details also merit attention, such as the way this following implies a radical departure from a former way of life. Simon and Andrew, for instance, follow Jesus by "leaving their nets" (1:18), while James and John, even more dramatically, leave their father and hired hands (1:20). In both cases Mark emphasizes the extent to which following Jesus involves a decisive break with the past. The new alignment dramatically transforms the old alignment, creating a new family centered on Jesus and his ministry (3:30–35).[5]

The initial stages of Jesus' ministry also reinforce the disciples' alignment with him through the introduction of other character groups by which Mark establishes the narrative's basic "role relationships."[6] The first of these new groups are the crowds attracted to Jesus' healing power.[7] It is precisely through implied contrasts to these crowds, especially in 1:21–45, that Mark's audience perceives the disciples' privileged access and service to their new leader. Simon, for instance, provides his own house as a base of operations for Jesus' ministry, if not also as a brief place of refuge when "the whole city" seeks out Jesus (1:32–34). Soon after this the disciples stand between Jesus and the crowds, pursuing the former on behalf of the latter, but ultimately following Jesus elsewhere for the sake of his stated mission (1:35–39). Thus the audience soon begins to understand the special place the disciples occupy in relation to Jesus. Though Jesus functions as the story's protagonist, his followers play a positive, assisting role in his outreach to those in need. Thus the promise of 1:17 appears to move swiftly to its full realization.

It is worth noting another significant, if not more fundamental, function of the crowds: they illustrate the extent to which God's invasive presence reverberates from region to region. Thus a common dynamic in these early episodes is the way in which Jesus' healing power attracts more and more people, often to the point of incredulity (1:28, 33, 45). Much like when John's preparation for "the way of the Lord" attracted "the whole Judean countryside and all the people of Jerusalem" (1:5), so now the Lord himself attracts hordes of people through his healing ministry. Of course those hordes, without access to Mark's theological discourse, lack the audience's fuller understanding of Jesus' significance. They flock to Jesus more out of sheer need than spiritual insight. Yet their consistent presence in the narrative's early chapters shows how God's transformative reign invades the world to real, human effect, bringing wholeness to the broken.[8]

Whereas 1:21–45 depicts the disciples' alignment with Jesus as he brings God's reign to the broken, 2:1–3:6 depicts their alignment with Jesus in his conflict with the powerful.[9] These traditional "leaders" of the people take the narrative stage in response to the sudden splash Jesus' ministry has created.[10] There is a decidedly theological dimension to their opposition, however, as it reveals the extent to which God's invasive action—both in its outreach to the marginalized and in its challenge to religious convention—elicits hostility from those purporting to uphold God's laws. This hostility first surfaces at 2:6–7 with the unspoken reaction of certain scribes when Jesus forgives a paralytic's sins: "Blasphemy! Who can forgive sins but God alone?" (2:7). It then continues, though now more openly and directly, in response to both Jesus' association with "tax collectors and sinners" (2:13–17) and his views on fasting (2:18–22). Finally, Jesus' iconoclastic interpretation of the Sabbath (2:27–28), which allows him to heal yet another person (3:1–5), results in a conspiracy by the Pharisees and Herodians to "destroy" him (3:6).

Although Jesus remains the primary focus of these debates, Mark makes crucial references to the disciples, implying their close alignment with him against his opponents. At 2:15–17, for instance, it is the disciples who receive the initial complaint that Jesus eats with sinners and tax collectors. Then, it is the action of the disciples—refraining from fasting (2:18–22) and plucking grain on the Sabbath (2:23–28)—that draws criticism, giving Jesus the opportunity to expound upon the significance of his ministry, with regard to both its newness (2:21–22) and its authority (2:27–28). In defending himself, then, Jesus also implicitly defends the actions of his disciples, thus suggesting a collective opposition to the leaders. In this way Mark's discourse gives the audience an altogether favorable impression of the disciples. For although they lack a real voice in the narrative, they nonetheless assist Jesus in his ministry and stand alongside him when that ministry meets sharp resistance.[11] Again, the promise of 1:17 seems to move toward swift fulfillment.

As the plot continues to unfold, Mark solidifies this sharp distinction between disciples aligned with Jesus on the one hand, and those opposed to him on the other hand. For soon after the Pharisees and Herodians conspire to kill him (3:6), Jesus forms a select group of twelve, the stated purpose of which is to "be with" him, to proclaim, and to have authority to cast out demons (3:14–15). As Suzanne Watts Henderson notes, "the disciples' significance lies not only in their nearness to Jesus marked by companionship and special instruction; it also lies . . . in the way he equips them to preach and to exercise authority to cast out demons—in a word, to do the things he does."[12] Understood in terms of Jesus' previous promise, it is an equipping of God's eschatological fishermen.

Though separated from the opposition's conspiracy by a short summary (3:7–12), the narrative placement of this equipping is crucial, for Mark has implicitly contrasted this "new solidarity"[13] with the hostility of the leaders. One group supports Jesus, while the other opposes him. Yet the contrast arises with one ominous, complicating factor since one of the Twelve, Judas Iscariot, is also named a betrayer (3:19). Here the audience receives its first clue that the solidarity of Jesus and his disciples will eventually falter, most likely in connection with the conspiracy just mentioned (3:6). A "handing over" (ὃς παρέδωκεν, 3:19) will link the two groups that now stand diametrically opposed.[14] Still, it is important to note that this foreshadowing refers to only one of the Twelve and does not appear to compromise the solidarity of the group in the present narrative moment.

Indeed, the issue of solidarity soon surfaces in Jesus' own teaching. For it is surely no coincidence that after the formation of this inner circle he gives another programmatic definition of his ministry as the earthly manifestation of a kingdom *un*divided. In response to the Jerusalem scribes who have accused him of collusion with Satan, Jesus challenges their presupposition: "If a kingdom is divided against itself, that kingdom is not able to stand. And if a house is divided against itself, that house will not be able to stand" (3:24–25). In other words, Jesus' power to cast out demons reflects his opposition to demons, not his alignment with them. Consequently, the audience may understand Jesus' entire ministry as the binding and plundering of those demonic forces, both human and spiritual, which have taken up residence in God's earthly "house."[15] Stated simply, God invades the world to exorcise the world—and now not only through Jesus but through his disciples as well.

This confrontation contains two levels of irony worth noting. First, Jesus' assertion of a united front against Satan carries dire consequences for his accusers. For it implies that they, precisely in their opposition to Jesus and his disciples, abet the cause of Satan (albeit unknowingly and indirectly). In addition to this, however, Jesus' parting shot on the dangers of blasphemy (3:28–29) implicates his opponents in that very transgression. For in accusing him of having an "unclean spirit" (3:30) they unknowingly blaspheme "against the Holy Spirit" (3:29) that he does have (1:10). Thus the Jerusalem scribes are partially correct—Jesus is possessed—but here the difference between partially and entirely correct is, ironically, the difference between blasphemy and reverence.[16] They have mistakenly denounced the "presence-of-God-come-too-near."[17]

Although Jesus directs his polemic toward the Jerusalem scribes, his words, particularly through the language of division, also bear upon the nature of his entire ministry, disciples included. This becomes clear when, immediately after the debate, Jesus draws an unmistakable line, at the expense of his own blood relatives (appropriately positioned "outside" Jesus' house), between insiders and outsiders: "Whoever does the will of God is my brother and sister and mother" (3:35). Mark's use of the relative pronoun "whoever" (ὅς) brings a distinctly universal flavor to this definition of "insider," a point reinforced by the fact that a "crowd" sits inside his house (3:32). Yet the audience also has every reason to believe, at this point in its narrative journey, that the disciples, more than any other characters, represent Jesus' true family. Called and equipped to extend God's eschatological reign into the world, they exemplify the new solidarity that Jesus intends.

Over a span of less than three chapters, then, Mark reinforces the audience's favorable expectations for Jesus' disciples in accordance with the promise of 1:17. They have gone from earthly fishermen to God's fishermen, endowed with Jesus' own "authority" (3:15). Therefore, although the narrative anticipates intense conflict between Jesus and worldly powers, the disciples appear on the appropriate side of the theological divide. Judas Iscariot is the foreboding exception.

Disciples as Insiders to God's Reign—or Not (4:1–34)

Having established a clear pattern of conflict, Mark proceeds at 4:1–34 to provide a reassuring clarification of the reign of God that Jesus proclaims and brings. This comes through a series of parables by which Jesus guarantees the consummation of that reign despite the multitude of earthly/demonic obstacles that appear in its way.[18] The parables also reinforce those boundaries Mark has already established between character groups, defining them now, however, in terms of their receptiveness to the "word" Jesus "sows"—their receptiveness to the transformative reign manifest in Jesus' ministry. Along these lines, 4:11–12 introduces the themes of divine revelation and concealment, forcing the audience to reevaluate character boundaries in terms of God's own transcendent action toward character groups. Generally speaking, "outsiders" now emerge as those from whom God withholds "the secret of God's reign" (τὸ μυστήριον τῆς βασιλείας τοῦ θεοῦ, 4:11), while the disciples appear, by virtue of their close alignment with Jesus, as insiders to whom that secret has been given. In a specific instance, however, Mark drops an ominous clue to the disciples' own blindness (4:13).

It is clear enough from Jesus' own words that his parables function as analogies for the transformative "reign of God" (4:11, 26, 30). With this connection in mind, it is also clear that the parables concede the existence of real and present obstacles to the full consummation of that reign. As Jesus himself explains, the word that he sows (i.e., his ministry) will frequently fail to take root, and for various reasons. Satan may take the word away as soon as someone hears it (4:15); the "trouble and persecution" that follows the word's sowing may cause others, despite their initial joy, to lose endurance and "fall away" (4:16–17); for still others, "the cares of the world and the lure of wealth" will choke the word Jesus sows in them (4:18–19). Indeed, by the time the audience arrives at the end of its narrative journey, it will have heard all three scenarios depicted.

Yet the plethora of seemingly insurmountable obstacles cannot take away from the fact that God's reign has, by virtue of Jesus' ministry, taken root. This means, in the words of Marcus, that "God's new age is arriving, *despite all evidence to the contrary*."[19] It is like a lamp, currently hidden under a basket, that will inevitably be disclosed (4:21–22), or like a mustard seed that begins as "the smallest of all the seeds" only to grow into "the greatest of all the shrubs" (4:30–32). In this way Jesus' present ministry, which attracts some while repelling others, represents only the firstfruits of a larger eschatological harvest. Characters in the story may not clearly see the encroachment of God's reign. Yet it is nonetheless there in incipient form; and Jesus, with divine authority, guarantees its future growth. As Juel notes, such assurances constitute "a forecast that keeps the audience's attention directed at the road ahead."[20]

But Jesus does not sugarcoat his assurances. Nor does he provide a timetable for the final consummation of God's reign. As with the prologue, then, hearers find themselves faced with a pronounced tension between present and future. While the prologue focused on a present time of fulfillment tempered by ominous clues of the future, however, the parables of 4:1–34 look to a future that will overturn the troubling circumstances of the present. They invite hearers to trust, despite considerable evidence to the contrary, that God's invasion will not limit itself to disparate "pockets" but rather will, in God's own time, fully encompass and transform the very world God has invaded.

How do the disciples factor into these promises? Although Jesus seems to leave the consummation of God's reign in God's own hands,[21] he has already promised, and even equipped, the disciples for extending that reign into the world. Within the narrative itself, then, Jesus' parables seek to reassure the disciples that their work as God's fishers, once it has begun, will meet the same kind of resistance that Jesus himself has met. Yet it is precisely because they are *God's* fishers that such resistance will not ultimately define their work. For God will give growth to the seeds they sow—"as if someone would scatter seed on the ground, and would sleep and rise night and day, and the seed would sprout, he does not know how" (4:26–7). In this way the parables of Mark 4 also reinforce the disciples' close alignment with Jesus, in contrast to other character groups (crowds and leaders) that lack the disciples' special eschatological vocation.

Thus when Jesus explains his sower parable (4:1–9) by using the language of insiders and outsiders, there is little question as to where the disciples stand: "When he was alone, those who were around him along with the twelve asked him about the parables. And he said to them, 'To you has been given the secret of God's reign. But for those outside everything comes in parables, in order that "in looking, they may look but not perceive, and in listening, they may listen but not understand—so that they may not turn again and be forgiven"'" (4:10–12).

The sharp contrast here between insiders and outsiders confirms what the audience has already inferred from previous episodes: the disciples have been granted a privileged place alongside Jesus, the agent of God's encroaching reign. What may very well surprise the audience, however, is God's own direct role in creating the insider/outsider distinction. For though many biblical scholars have tried to soften the logic of 4:12,[22] its plain grammatical sense suggests that the difference between insiders and outsiders hardly results from narrative chips falling randomly where they may. It is rather intended: "in order that" (ἵνα, 4:12). If one adds to this implied intention that Jesus also quotes directly from Isa. 6:9–10, one begins to see the makings of a divine strategy. God's commissioning of Isaiah to speak a hardening word to Israel parallels the commissioning of Jesus to speak in parables to "those outside."[23] There is a sense, then, in which Mark 4:12 expresses "not so much the intent of Jesus as the will of God recorded in the Scriptures."[24]

Thus amid the chaos of God's eschatological invasion of the world (through Jesus), God's transcendent action (apart from Jesus) now begins to emerge more clearly. The reality of God's encroaching reign bypasses people, not because they lack or misuse the faculties of perceiving and understanding, but rather because God conceals it from them. Moreover, Mark depicts this concealment as God's long anticipated scriptural will. Though Mark balances this concealment with reassuring promises of revelation—"nothing is hidden except to be made manifest" (4:22)[25]—it nonetheless remains a surprising, if not disturbing, reality in the present narrative moment.

Jesus' appropriation of Isa. 6:9–10 also has significant implications for the way Mark's audience understands and experiences its overall narrative journey. For although Mark 4:12 pertains most directly to a specific scene—Jesus teaching crowds by the lakeshore—the theological effect of his private explanation, much like the chapter as a whole, has a rippling effect that moves both backward and forward through the narrative. On the one hand, then, Jesus' explanation marks a significant reshaping of the audience's memory, as the possibility of God concealing his own reign forces a retrospective reflection: Has this been happening from the beginning of the narrative? On the other hand, 4:12 significantly alters the audience's expectations of what will come, so that the possibility of divine concealment accompanies the audience from this point forward, affecting its experience of the rest of Jesus' ministry. In both cases Mark does not answer such questions but simply raises them.

In this way 4:12 functions less as a "massive inconsistency"[26] within some static Markan logic than as a surprising development in the Markan plot. Granted, Jesus' private explanation need not necessarily apply to the entirety of his ministry; Mark does not force his audience to see in all events the effects of divine concealment. He does, however, introduce a new and significant theological possibility that, once established, cannot be ignored. No longer may an audience attribute character confusion exclusively to the fact that Jesus urges secrecy with some[27] or speaks privately to others.[28] Nor may it attribute such confusion simply to the nature of Mark's discourse, that is, to the fact that Mark privileges the audience at the expense of the characters. For 4:12 gives the audience an altogether different angle from which to evaluate and experience Mark's Gospel, a thoroughly theological angle from which human confusion and eschatological invasion actually come from the same God.

With respect to the disciples 4:12 also reinforces, at least momentarily, their insider status vis-à-vis Jesus and God's invasive action through him. In the first place, it is a private explanation ("when he was alone," 4:10) directed primarily, if not exclusively, to the disciples ("those who were around him along with the twelve," 4:10).[29] As with previous scenes, then, Mark sets the disciples apart from large crowds (4:1) that follow Jesus. In addition, however, Jesus' explanation introduces the notion that "seeing and not seeing, hearing and not hearing are God's business,"[30] that is, the disciples' insider status "is not dependent on superior mental qualities."[31] It is rather a direct consequence of divine action. Thus the God whose eschatological reign invades the world via Jesus is also the God who both reveals and conceals, pulling a select few inside, while leaving the rest outside.[32]

Were Mark's narrative to end here, after only four chapters, the audience would walk away understanding, as clearly as the distinction of 4:11, that Jesus' disciples will remain insiders by virtue of God's own revealing activity. Viewed from this angle, one might well characterize the Markan disciples using the Matthean Jesus, who, in reply to Peter's messianic confession, exclaims, "Blessed are you, Simon son of Jonah! For flesh and blood has not revealed this to you, but my Father in heaven" (Matt. 16:17). Mark, however, will guide his audience down a rather different narrative path, as subsequent chapters depict the disciples' consistent misunderstanding of Jesus' ministry (4:41; 6:35, 49–50, 52; 7:17; 8:4, 17), their repeated resistance to Jesus' fate (8:22–10:52), and their troubling abandonment of Jesus in his final hours (14:26–15:47).

Interestingly, such misunderstanding first surfaces (though somewhat fleetingly) immediately after 4:10–12. Having explained his use of parables in terms of divine concealment, Jesus quickly finds out that his companions need the sower parable explained to them. Thus his surprised response: "Do you not understand this parable? Then how will you know all the parables?" (4:13). An attentive audience notices the irony of these rhetorical questions in that Jesus directs them to the very people he has just deemed insiders, presumably by virtue of their understanding.

How does one explain this lack of understanding on the part of the disciples? With respect to the narrative discourse it functions simply as a kind of narrative segue, giving Mark the opportunity to move the audience from the opening parable (4:1–9) to an explanation (4:14–20) and to smaller clarifying parables (4:21–34).[33] Within the narrative itself it also underlines Jesus' own vested interest in the disciples' comprehension and his willingness to teach them. It is as if the disciples "hear Jesus and are given the understanding that they cannot achieve on their own."[34]

I question, however, whether these approaches to 4:13 (despite their obvious insights) do not underestimate the rhetorical force of Jesus' question, the implied answer to which is, given Jesus' own reliability, yes. That Jesus' closest followers need an explanation indicates a failure to understand that catches even Jesus off guard. Thus he does not move to an immediate explanation but pauses to call attention to the incomprehension itself, clarifying the high stakes involved: "Then how will you know all the parables?" That Jesus must explain his parable to his own disciples, then, does not necessarily serve to highlight their insider status. Yes, Jesus proves willing to bring them inside; but he also expects them already to be there. From his perspective things clearly are not as they should be.

This first indication of disciple incomprehension, along with Jesus' own befuddled response, begins the steady emergence of what Robert Hamerton-Kelly calls "the irony of the excluded insider."[35] This is not to say that such irony will resonate fully with the audience at this particular narrative moment (though it certainly may); and it is even less likely that such a brief reference to incomprehension would negate, in a single instance, the cumulative effect of Mark's first three chapters, which consistently reinforce the disciples' insider status. The remainder of Mark's narrative will, however, intensify this "irony of the excluded insider," causing 4:13 to echo more forcefully in the audience's collective memory. Thus hearers will gradually learn what is now only implied, that the calling and equipping of the disciples as God's fishers does not guarantee their understanding of Jesus' ministry. Indeed, as the audience's confidence in the disciples slowly wanes so too does its confidence in the swift realization of Jesus' initial promise to them (1:17), along with its confidence in God willing such a swift realization.

EMERGING RIFT WITH JESUS (4:35–8:22)

The Disciples' Faithlessness and Fear (4:35–6:6)

In the very next scene (4:35–41) Mark's audience begins to experience the slow but steady disintegration of the disciples' close alignment with Jesus. Having set out across the sea together (4:35–36), a "great storm" arises, threatening to flood the boat (4:37). Mark contrasts the understandable panic of the disciples with the perplexing calm of Jesus: the followers fear for their lives, while their leader sleeps peacefully (4:39).[36] Once aroused from his slumber, Jesus "rebukes" the wind with the same authoritative command that characterizes both his healings (1:25, 41; 2:5, 11) and his original summons to the disciples (1:17, 20; 2:14): "Quiet! Be still!" (4:39). Based on the immediate calming (obedience?) of the storm, Mitzi Minor notes how "Jesus has done what, in the Hebrew Bible, only God can do."[37] Possessed by God's own Spirit, he has exercised authority over the creation itself.

It is with Jesus' subsequent reprimand that the disciples appear in a negative light: "Why are you afraid? Do you not yet have faith?" (4:40). The easily overlooked adverb οὔπω ("not yet") prevents the audience from limiting this lack of faith to the present narrative moment. Instead it is pushed by Jesus to entertain the possibility of a faithless state that the present moment has only now made manifest. Even as a mere possibility, this reinforces the scenario suggested by Jesus' first critical questioning of the disciples: "Do you not understand . . . ?" (4:13). Such questions, coming from the lips of the narrative's authoritative protagonist, exercise a cumulative effect upon the audience, raising the specter of a potential rift. As if to acknowledge this specter, Mark quickly alludes to the disciples' collective ignorance of Jesus' identity. "Who is this," they ask, "that even the wind and sea obey him?" (4:41). It is a question that closely resembles the reactions of the astonished crowds (1:27) and authorities (2:7)—those whom Jesus has recently labeled outsiders (4:11).

Having finally crossed the sea (5:1), the disciples fade somewhat from the narrative spotlight. This does not mean, however, that Mark's subsequent narration has no bearing on the audience's estimation of them. For instance, the healing of the Gerasene demoniac (5:1–20) makes clear that the invasion of God's eschatological reign does not depend on the disciples. Jesus continues to engage, and prevail, in the apocalyptic battle against demons. At the same time, Mark shows how this overcoming of demonic forces, viewed favorably from the audience's privileged vantage point, meets resistance from various characters in the story. Much like the disciples' reaction to Jesus' storm quelling, the restoration of the demoniac evokes fear from local residents (5:15), so much that they beg Jesus to leave the area (5:17).[38] Just as God's disturbance of the natural order elicits fear from Jesus' followers, so God's disturbance of the natural order—and, perhaps more significantly, the status quo[39]—elicits fear from nonfollowers.

The subsequent intercalation of two healing episodes (5:21–43) also has implications for how the audience evaluates the disciples in relation to God's action. Here too the audience sees that the invasion of God's reign does not depend upon the disciples' understanding. Indeed, the healing of the hemorrhaging woman suggests that, to a certain extent, it does not depend even on Jesus' understanding. For when the woman approaches Jesus in a crowd of people, the mere touching of his cloak stops her twelve-year bleeding (5:27–29). Realizing only that power has left his body, Jesus asks, "Who touched my clothes?" (5:30). While the leader proves ignorant only of the woman's identity, however, his followers prove ignorant of the entire situation. "You see the crowd pressing upon you," the disciples exclaim, "so how can you say, 'Who touched me?'" (5:31). With respect to both Jesus and his disciples, God's invasive action overcomes the limitations of its human agents.

The healing episodes of 5:21–43 also serve as positive foils against which the audience may gauge the disciples. The audience will remember that, on the initial voyage across the sea, Jesus chastised the disciples for "not yet" having faith (4:40). How ironic, then, that Jesus here encounters faith from two nonfollowers. When the hemorrhaging woman identifies herself, Jesus immediately recognizes what was missing among his disciples: "Daughter, your faith has healed you" (5:34). Likewise, in response to Jairus's anxiety over his daughter's death, Jesus exclaims, "Do not fear, only have faith" (5:36). Admitting a certain degree of ambiguity, it seems that Jesus here encourages Jairus to maintain, in the face of apparent loss, the same trust that underlay his original petition to Jesus (5:23). Regardless of the precise implication, however, one hears at 5:36 a direct echo of 4:40–41, where Jesus contrasts the disciples' "fear" with their lack of "faith."[40]

A similar lack of faith surfaces in the next episode (6:1–6), when the residents of Jesus' hometown prove unable to reconcile the authority of his words and actions with his humble beginnings. Instead, as Mark explains, "they took offense at him" (ἐσκανδαλίζοντο ἐν αὐτῷ, 6:3), a response that Jesus interprets in light of scriptural precedent: "A prophet is not without honor, except in his hometown and among his own kin" (6:4). Thus the people of Nazareth react in accordance with the well-known theological pattern, repeated throughout Scripture, by which God's prophet meets rejection from the prophet's (and God's) own people.[41] Moreover, Mark implies that this "faithlessness" (ἀπιστία), which elicits Jesus' own amazement (6:6), prevents him from continuing his healing ministry in this area, at least with the effectiveness that the audience has come to expect.[42]

It is worth repeating that all of these scenes, in their depictions of faith, faithlessness, and fear, come to bear upon the audience's estimation of the disciples even though they do not really factor in the scenes themselves. This would not be the case, of course, had Mark not previously made reference to the disciples' own faithlessness and fear (4:40–41). In making such a reference, however, he sets up comparisons and contrasts in subsequent scenes that repeat those themes. Thus the hemorrhaging woman exhibits not only faith but the very faith absent in the disciples. Jairus is encouraged to overcome not only fear but the very fear exhibited by the disciples (albeit fear under different circumstances). Keeping in mind the potential for such subtexts, Mark's audience will find the dynamic of the Nazareth synagogue perhaps the most disturbing of all, since it shows that faithlessness can lead to an outright rejection of Jesus. Thus, while the audience can only be encouraged at the extension of God's reign through the ministry of Jesus, it must come to terms with the potential breakdown of the disciples in their solidarity with Jesus. The specter of a rift still hovers over the narrative.

The Hopeful Side of the Tension (6:7–44)

Given the specter of a rift, it is likely no coincidence that the next episodes (6:7–44) provide a hopeful, though short-lived, portrait of the disciples. Here the audience comes to see that the potential exists—within God and/or the disciples (Mark does not specify)—for the disciples, despite their own fearful lack of faith, to extend God's eschatological reign into the world. They can be fishers of people. Since the audience cannot erase the troubling effect of 4:35–6:6, however, it must hold these positive episodes in tension with the episodes immediately preceding them. In other words, the audience's memory of previous events does not yield or succumb to present events; rather, it shapes and is shaped by those events. In the specific case of 6:7–44, then, the audience sees that God's encroaching reign will not be impeded by human obstacles.

When Jesus commissions the Twelve to extend his ministry into the world (6:7–13), Mark gives the audience its most substantive view yet of how Jesus' promise at 1:17 will be fulfilled. Appropriately, the scene echoes the creation of the Twelve at 3:13–19, not only in its focus on the "apostles"[43] but also in the parallel it draws between their ministry and the ministry of Jesus. In particular, Mark depicts once again the bestowal of Jesus' divine authority: "He gave to them authority over the unclean spirits" (6:7; cf. 1:21–28; 11:27–33). In addition to this, however, the proclamation of the Twelve, with its emphasis on repentance (6:12), echoes Jesus' programmatic proclamation of God's reign ("Repent and believe the good news," 1:15), while the brief summary of their success confirms tangible results: "And they cast out many demons, and anointed with oil many who were sick and healed them" (6:13). Thus, unlike the account of their creation at 3:13–19, here the Twelve are *employed* for God's purposes. It is the first instance of God's transformative reign encroaching through agents other than Jesus. The disciples are finally fishers of people.

Yet in terms of discourse time (the time actually devoted to narrating these events[44]), the disciples' successful mission is short-lived. Indeed, as Fowler rightly notes, Mark's brief description (6:12–13) withholds more information than it gives.[45] By contrast, hearers find a much more elaborate account of John the Baptist's execution by Herod (6:14–29), a scene sandwiched ominously between the commission (6:7–13) and return (6:30–31) of the Twelve. As a result of this intercalation, the audience may begin to link violent political resistance to the ministry of the Twelve—a connection that will soon implicate all of Jesus' disciples.[46] In other words, Mark suggests, through his sequencing of events, that the extension of God's reign into the world will meet opposition from those wielding worldly power. The attentive audience will remember the equally ominous reference to John's arrest in conjunction with the beginning of Jesus' public ministry (1:14), as well as the subtle parallel drawn, through the repetition of the phrase ὀπίσω μου ("behind me," 1:7, 17) between Jesus and the disciples in this regard.[47] So at 6:14–29 the audience sees in grotesque detail the consequences of John's arrest, though now in close narrative proximity to the beginning of the disciples' public ministry. Thus it seems that to be a fisher of people is to risk losing one's life (foreshadowing 8:34–35).

In this way the mission of the Twelve, both in its successful results and in its troubling undertones, closely aligns the disciples once again with Jesus. Mark depicts this alignment rather explicitly at the conclusion of the Twelve's journey, when Jesus instructs them to accompany him privately to a deserted place for rest (6:31). This retreat resembles the original appointing of the Twelve atop a secluded mountain (3:13), a scene that followed the first explicitly narrated conspiracy against Jesus (3:6). Much like those earlier events, here Mark aligns the disciples (specifically the Twelve) with Jesus and thus, by way of association, with the encroachment of God's reign into the world (as well as the consequences of that encroachment). Along with Jesus they act as agents of God's invasive action and, consequently, as (future) victims of worldly hostility.

This positive alignment continues when the searching crowds manage to find Jesus and the disciples despite their attempts at solitude. The deserted place (6:31) in which Jesus proceeds to teach the crowds provides an appropriate backdrop for the Gospel's first miraculous feeding account. In particular, as scholars have long noted, Jesus' "wilderness" feeding echoes God's own provision for the Israelites.[48] Here, however, divine sustenance comes via the disciples, whom Jesus empowers to distribute a meager supply of bread and fish to five thousand people. Mark even depicts the disciples' compassionate concern for the hungry crowds (6:35–36), echoing Jesus' own compassion (6:34).[49] Although the disciples show initial confusion over Jesus' intentions ("You give them something to eat," 6:37), such confusion does not prevent the ultimate realization of those intentions; nor does it necessarily reflect poorly on the disciples, given their understandable inability to read Jesus' mind.[50] Thus the audience comes to find that the realization of God's purpose does not depend upon the disciples' ability to understand that purpose, even when it is the disciples themselves who realize it. One might even say that the disciples prove successful fishers of people despite themselves.

God's Hardening Revealed (6:45–8:21)

As the audience nears the midpoint of its narrative journey it encounters an interspersion of both positive and negative depictions of the disciples. Within this section, however, it also stumbles across a significant theological development: the revelation of God's hardening of the disciples (6:52; 8:17). Given the repetition of these hardening references within the span of only two chapters, it is difficult for the audience to dismiss them simply as narrative anomalies. Instead, it is forced to consider the extent to which previous instances of the disciples' misunderstanding stem from the very God who calls them and acts through them for his eschatological purposes.

This divine hardening first surfaces in a second boat scene (6:45–52), as Mark moves to a setting in which the disciples do not tend to fare very well: the lake (cf. 4:35–41). Here Jesus, having dismissed the now well-fed crowd, instructs his disciples to venture across the lake to Bethsaida (6:45). Then, after spending some time alone in prayer (thus implying God's transcendence vis-à-vis the Son), Jesus himself crosses by "walking on the sea" (6:46–48). Much like the first boat scene (4:35–41), the disciples respond to Jesus' miraculous act with confusion and fear: "they thought he was a ghost, and they cried out, for they all saw him and were terrified"(6:50a). As expected, however, Jesus addresses this deficient response directly: "Take courage! I am. Do not fear" (6:50b). The common translation ἐγώ εἰμι as "It is I"[51] misses a likely allusion to God's own self-revelation to Moses and Israel ("I am").[52] Thus Mark's scripturally astute hearers find not only words of assurance from Jesus but an important theological disclosure: the disciples express fear in the face of God's own presence. Or, viewed from a different angle, the great "I am" elicits fear in those whom he encounters.

Mark's use of the phrase "I am" intimately connects Jesus and God, reinforcing God's invasive mode of action. At the same time, Mark's allusion to the disciples' fear (6:50)—a trait that Mark casts in a predominantly negative light (4:41; 5:15, 36)[53]—reinforces their negative characterization vis-à-vis Jesus.

What is altogether new to the narrative, however, is the subsequent reference to God's concealing activity. For according to Mark's own commentary the disciples' fear and confusion stems ultimately from the fact that "their heart was hardened" (6:52), a condition that has also rendered them incapable of understanding "about the loaves" (6:52) in the previous episode.[54] In terms of grammar, the perfect passive construction of the participle (πεπωρωμένη) suggests both a completed activity and an activity of which the disciples function as objects. It is what scholars frequently call a "divine passive."[55] The disciples have been acted upon by God, who has hardened their collective "heart" (the singular noun καρδία) against a proper understanding of Jesus in the story.

It seems appropriate that Mark employs hardening language given the previous scene's echoes of the exodus story, in which God not only provided for the Israelites in the wilderness (like Jesus and the disciples at 6:30–44) but also delivered them from bondage through the hardening of Pharaoh's heart.[56] Viewed from this angle, Mark's reference to divine hardening in the second boat scene (6:40–44) demonstrates his skill in incorporating scriptural themes into his Gospel. However, to limit one's focus simply to Mark's scriptural context misses the significance of that context for the interpretation of Mark's own narrative. One cannot dismiss the significance of God having hardened the *disciples'* hearts simply by appealing to its thematic "appropriateness" with respect to Mark's scriptural allusions. Rather, one must come to terms with that hardening as a significant factor in the shaping of Mark's plot.

If we follow this line of thought, the reference to hardening picks up the theme of divine concealment first introduced at 4:11–12, a passage in which Jesus explains his parables, with reference to Isa. 6:9–10, as God's intention to withhold "understanding" (συνίημι, Mark 4:12; 6:52a) from "those outside" (4:11).[57] It is the second allusion to divine concealment that prevents comprehension. Here, however, the narrative connects such concealment directly to the disciples, without the ambiguity hearers experienced at 4:13. In clarifying this theological possibility, 6:52 thus becomes a watershed in the audience's narrative journey. God not only extends his eschatological reign through the disciples but also hardens them so that they do not understand Jesus. Moreover, without the requisite understanding the disciples express fear, a disposition Mark has already twice contrasted with faith (4:40–41; 5:36).

Equally important is that Mark reveals God's hardening via direct commentary to his audience. This means, on the one hand, that the disciples presumably have no knowledge of God's action toward them. Yet it also raises the possibility, on the other hand, that Jesus lacks such knowledge as well. If that is the case, then 6:47–52 would depict a remarkable irony between Jesus' self-designation as the great "I am" walking on water and his limited insights into the struggles of his own followers. It would also stand in contrast to previous displays of near-omniscient perception, such as when Jesus communicates with demons (1:23–26, 34; 3:11; 5:6–13), feels the single touch of a woman in a crowd (5:27–32), and understands the inner thoughts of his opponents (2:1–12; 3:5). Has Mark, then, provided an unexpected window into the limits of Jesus' knowledge? The question remains open until the narrative provides further clarification.

Mark quickly leaves behind the possibility of divine hardening and returns instead to a familiar narrative dynamic. The brief summary of Jesus' immense popularity in Gennesaret, where "that whole region" (6:55) flocks to him, echoes his initial successes in Galilee (1:32–34; 3:7–12). Moreover, the ensuing debate between Jesus and the Pharisees over cleanliness laws (7:1–23) resembles the earlier debate scenes (2:1–3:6), particularly in that Jesus' opponents challenge him indirectly by criticizing his disciples (7:2; cf. 2:19, 23–24). Through these more positive scenes (which continue through two more healing episodes at 7:24–37), Mark reintroduces, however briefly, the alignment between Jesus and his followers over against the leaders. Thus the encroachment of God's reign continues, attracting the broken while repelling the powerful. The key difference in this case, however, is that the audience now hears this dynamic over the echo of divine hardening at 6:52. Consequently, it must begin to wrestle with an emerging tension by which God not only challenges the disciples (indirectly, through Jesus) to understand (4:13; 7:18) but also *causes* them (directly, through hardening) to misunderstand.[58]

Although Mark does not dwell on God's hardening at 6:52, it does not take him long to return to it, and this time with more theological force. The more encouraging, and much more familiar, dynamic of 6:53–7:24 quickly changes during and after a second miraculous feeding (8:1–10), in which the disciples again fail to understand Jesus' capacity to provide (8:4). What was a rather understandable ignorance in the first feeding episode (6:33–44) here turns decidedly negative, not only because it is the second such scenario (in which the disciples are expected to remember lessons from the first) but also because the disciples now face fewer people and more plentiful resources.[59] Moreover, having since heard of the potential for God to harden the disciples, the audience now faces deeper questions about the source of this ignorance. The prospect of divine concealment now looms over the story. Thus, even though Jesus again employs the disciples to miraculous ends, the rift between them ("How is one able to feed these people?" 8:4) now appears considerably more complex—even mysterious. The disciples' confusion may stem from something much larger than their own ineptitude.[60]

With this second and more perplexing feeding story resonating with the audience, Mark begins to accentuate the sense of divine mystery. When the Pharisees arrive on the scene to "test" Jesus by asking him for a sign from heaven

(8:11), Jesus refuses the request, insisting that "a sign will not be given to this generation" (8:12). Then, having departed with the disciples by boat (8:13), he proceeds to warn the disciples about future testing: "Look! Beware of the yeast of the Pharisees and of the yeast of Herod" (8:15). The disciples misinterpret this bread metaphor, saying to one another, "It is because we have no bread" (8:14). Apparently unappreciative (or simply misunderstanding) Jesus' potential for miraculous provision, they take from the second feeding only a lesson in proper preparation. This at least is how Jesus understands their confusion, for his scolding response attempts to clarify his power of provision (8:17–21).

It is at the beginning of this reprimand that the theme of divine concealment reemerges: "Why are you talking about not having bread? Do you still not perceive or understand? Do you have hearts that have been hardened? Having eyes, do you not see? And having ears, do you not hear? And do you not remember?" (8:17–18; cf. 4:12). Mark's use of the verb συνίημι ("understand," 8:17, 21) takes the audience back to Jesus' words at 6:52 and 4:12. More significantly, however, Jesus' description of the disciples failing to see despite having eyes, and failing to hear despite having ears, directly echoes Jesus description of "those outside" at 4:11–12. Furthermore, as if to underline the theological significance of this connection, Mark once again notes the disciples' hardened hearts (πεπωρωμένην ἔχετε τὴν καρδίαν ὑμῶν, 8:17). The echoing of the "divine passive" from 6:52 places the theme of hardening alongside the theme of blindness/dumbness, creating a more elaborate picture of God's transcendent action vis-à-vis the disciples.

Yet is this necessarily *God's* activity?

There are two major alternatives for interpreting 8:17–18, but they are alternatives that, in my view, share some questionable presuppositions that preclude the consideration of crucial theological details in the larger narrative. The first alternative hears these verses as a reference to self-hardening, so that the disciples essentially bring their own condition upon themselves. This approach takes seriously that Jesus tries to hold the disciples accountable for their own incomprehension, concluding from that fact that misunderstanding leads to hardened hearts, and not vice versa.[61] It does not, however, take into sufficient account that both references to hardening use passive verbs and thus imply an outside acting agent. That is, the disciples' hearts are not merely "hard," like the leaders who oppose Jesus (3:5), but *have been hardened*— presumably by someone or something.

The second alternative explains these verses as a cloaked reference to Satan, a character Jesus has already mentioned as an obstacle to his ministry (3:20–30; 4:15) and whom he will soon connect explicitly to the disciples' misunderstanding (8:33). This approach takes seriously the passive voice of Mark's hardening verbs (6:52; 8:17) and simply posits Satan as the most logical candidate for an outside acting agent.[62] It does not, however, account sufficiently for the fact that Mark connects Satan with *testing* (1:13; 8:33), not hardening, while the exodus tradition (with which Mark is surely familiar) connects God with hardening. Moreover, as God's initial casting of Jesus into the wilderness (1:12–13) shows, even divine and satanic purposes can intersect in mysterious ways, so that this approach to 8:17–18 hardly lets God off the proverbial hook.[63]

More to the point, both of these alternatives share a common presupposition: the disciples' misunderstanding can stem only from a single cause. Advocates of these approaches assume that the text can have only one meaning. Operating out of this presupposition, they then interpret based on the more theologically driven assumption that a strict—and in fact unbreakable—cognitive alignment must exist between Jesus and the Markan narrator, whose "omniscience" allows him to report the activities of God in the story. Yet while Mark's discourse indicates a significant cognitive alignment between Jesus and God,[64] and while that alignment certainly gives rise to remarkable spiritual insight on the part of Jesus, it does not necessarily follow that Jesus, as a character in the story, will *always* reap the benefits of the narrator's perspective. Though certainly a superhuman character, particularly insofar as God's own Spirit possesses him, Jesus remains a character nonetheless. Thus the possibility always exists for Mark to privilege the audience even at Jesus' expense, especially since God functions transcendently as well.

That Jesus holds the disciples accountable for their incomprehension does not, therefore, mean that the audience must view things in the same black-and-white terms. Indeed, once the above hermeneutic presupposition is removed, the possibility of divine hardening becomes quite real, even though it emerges over the course of several chapters. It is a cumulative argument, beginning with the acknowledgment that God acts, or can potentially act, within the narrative. The ironic placement of 4:13 ("Do you not understand this parable?") after 4:11–12 first opens up the possibility, however implicit, of the disciples' being targets of divine concealment. The explicit mention of their hardened "heart" at 6:52 reinforces this possibility in language reminiscent of God's role in the exodus story. Thus 8:17 simply repeats the assertion of 6:52—and in language echoing 4:11–12.[65]

Jesus' exasperated reproach should not, therefore, prompt the audience to preclude God's complicity in the growing rift. Rather, it simply triggers an awareness that Mark has privileged the audience vis-à-vis Jesus—at least with respect to the specific issue of God's hardening. By virtue of this privileging, hearers of the narrative gauge the disciples' incomprehension much differently than Jesus gauges it inside the narrative. From the vantage point of the audience benefiting from Mark's discourse, a subtle yet significant friction now seems to exist (again, over the specific issue of the disciples' misunderstanding) between God's action toward the disciples on the one hand, and Jesus' reprimand of the disciples on the other hand.

To support this claim, it is worth noting that a similar dynamic occurs toward the end of the narrative, during Jesus' Gethsemane prayer: "Abba, Father, for you all things are possible. Take from me this cup. Yet not what I want but what you want" (14:36). Though Mark does not "privilege" his hearers in this scene, he does illustrate, however fleetingly, a similar tension in the relationship between Father and Son. Though the former literally possesses the latter, and though the latter speaks and acts authoritatively on behalf of the former, the audience here finds Jesus suggesting a fate different than the one he has previously deemed "necessary" (δεῖ, 8:31; cf. 9:31; 10:33–34). As Kevin Madigan notes, Jesus' Gethsemane prayer "is striking because of his vehement resistance to the divine will rather than his quiet surrender to it."[66] The eventual submission to the divine will ("yet not what I want but what you want") does not erase the significant tension implied by the original petition ("take from me this cup"). Rather, the petition reinforces the significance of the submission, showing the audience that such submission comes in spite of reservation (though also, perhaps, by virtue of Jesus' own possession by God).[67]

Thus Jesus does not in every case fall into perfect alignment with the omniscience of God and with the Markan narrator, who depicts them both.[68] To be sure, Mark exercises considerable restraint in depicting such dissonance—and for good reason. For Jesus' ultimate alignment with God ensures the trustworthiness of his "gospel of God" (1:14), and it is the narrative means by which Mark depicts God's eschatological invasion of the world. I agree, then, with the overwhelming consensus among interpreters, "By the time Jesus first speaks to announce that the rule of God has arrived, the reader is prepared to trust whatever he says and does."[69] This basic premise need not preclude, however, the possibility of tension, however subtle, between Jesus and God (as 14:36 shows most clearly). Of course, were Mark to reinforce this tension throughout his Gospel the audience would have reason to question Jesus' reliability as God's spokesperson, if not also the extent to which Jesus' ministry truly manifests God's reign. Arising at only a handful of moments, however, the tension actually serves Mark's theological purpose, illustrating how God, as the story's primary actor, not only invades the story world but, to a certain extent, authors it. It is the very tension Mark's hearers experience at the climax of the narrative: "My God, my God, why have you forsaken me?" (15:34).

It is also worth noting that the tension of Mark 8:17 does not ultimately undermine Jesus' reliability, since his questions ironically express the truth. While his amazement is quite genuine, his scathing questions suggest their own answers, at least for the audience: Yes, the disciples still fail to perceive and understand. Yes, their hearts have been hardened. Yes, they have eyes yet fail to see, and ears yet fail to hear. In this way the incredulous Jesus actually reinforces what hearers already know, or have at least seriously considered, based on Mark's previous commentary (6:52). For the audience, then, it is not simply a matter of the disciples' acting "contrary to Jesus' intentions."[70] It is, more fundamentally, a matter of God's mysterious workings in the lives of both parties.

CONCLUSION

The first half of Mark's Gospel develops two interrelated tensions. The first has been a constant source of deliberation for modern scholars, namely, the tension between expectation and reality as it pertains to Jesus' disciples. For while the first four chapters draw the disciples into close alignment with Jesus, the second four depict a growing rift. Even as God proves capable of employing the disciples as fishers of people, those instances are short-lived and increasingly overshadowed by the fracture within Jesus' "family." The audience must therefore reevaluate its initial expectations, expectations originating at 1:17 and reinforced by the positive momentum of the first four chapters. As Tannehill notes: "If we think in terms of consistent but static doctrine, there may seem to be a conflict between this positive view of the disciples and other material in Mark. If we think in terms of narrative development, however, we have the common story technique of encouraging the reader to contemplate one possibility so that he will feel more sharply the opposite development when it arrives."[71]

In coming to terms with this "opposite development," scholars generally follow Jesus' lead in holding the disciples' accountable for their own incomprehension. This is especially the case as one's interpretive focus moves deeper into the narrative, that is, after it is clear that such incomprehension is not simply an anomaly but rather an emerging problem. Thus, although an audience might empathize with the disciples' fear in first witnessing Jesus' power over nature (4:35–41), it will be less inclined to empathize four chapters later. Mark's inclusion of two miraculous feeding stories (as opposed to one) plays a crucial role in this evolving perspective, since it prohibits the audience from attributing the disciples' misunderstanding to altogether new experiences. It shows that even repetition does not help them. Practice does not make perfect. Thus the audience understands Jesus' growing consternation, and perhaps even shares his amazement, when he finally asks, "Do you not yet understand?" (8:21).

Yet what scholars have largely overlooked, in my view, is God's own role in this development and, more specifically, the way God's divergent modes of action prevent any single explanation for it. With respect to God's invasive action, for instance, it is not enough to say simply that the disciples misunderstand *Jesus*, for the very things Jesus does to elicit their confusion he does by virtue of his possession by God's Spirit. For all its ambiguity and tension, the first half of the narrative is rather consistent on this point: the disciples' misunderstanding arises in response to the greatest of Jesus' miracles, that is, to his Godlike authority in matters of nature (4:35–41; 6:45–52) and provision (6:30–44; 8:1–10, 14–22). The disciples misunderstand those events that set Jesus apart from a mere healer, the very deeds that powerfully illustrate (for the audience at least) the encroachment of God's eschatological reign into the world.

To say only that the disciples misunderstand Jesus, then, is to miss a more fundamental theological point: God confounds the disciples. In this way the disciples resemble the Gospel's minor characters who, also lacking the benefit of Mark's prologue, can respond to Jesus based only on their varying and limited perspectives of him. This does not necessarily excuse their misunderstanding, however, since it is precisely the disciples who receive added windows into Jesus' Godlike powers. Jesus has even clarified for them, in private, that his ministry incipiently manifests God's reign while the surrounding crowds receive only parables (4:11–12). In this way the disciples face the challenge of recognizing Jesus' significance as the agent of God's reign and, consequently, the significance of their own vocation as the collective extension of Jesus' ministry (secondary agents in a sense). It is precisely because of this promised vocation (1:17; 13:9–13) that the audience, holding its own vested interest in the disciples, can empathize with Jesus' effort to "bring them to repentance"[72] and thus "*keep* their hearts from being hardened."[73]

Yet this accounts for only one side of the Gospel's underlying theological tension. For with respect to God's transcendent action one finds that the growing rift stems not from the disciples' ineptitude but rather from divine hardening. It is a hardening, moreover, that runs against the grain of Jesus' own expectations, thus prohibiting the audience from blaming the disciples to the degree that Jesus himself does (even as that same audience empathizes with his concern). I hope I have made this argument sufficient already. What I would like to clarify here, however, is how exactly this dimension of the narrative creates tension and does not simply override the alternative perspective. If God does harden the disciples, what other explanation is needed? Why not simply let the disciples off the hook completely?

I admit that this question does not invite easy answers. In my view, however, God's hardening creates tension precisely because God continues to act invasively. In this chapter I have perhaps given a disproportionate emphasis to God's hardening in an effort to counter the scholarly tendency to overlook it. But I would not want to distort the larger picture. For the audience experiences the encroachment of God's transformative reign in every person who is healed, in every crowd that is fed, and in every storm that is stilled. More to the point, the audience experiences this encroachment even in the actions of the disciples, albeit fleetingly and with misunderstanding. The narrative gives an overriding sense of divine invasion, such that a few references to divine hardening/concealment will not override it. As Tannehill astutely notes, Mark's Gospel is a narrative with development, not a container of "static doctrine." Thus it does not compel hearers toward a single explanation but creates a temporal and dynamic experience. To the extent, then, that God continues to act *both* transcendently *and* invasively, the growing rift between Jesus and his disciples will reflect that very tension.

To support this claim it is worth noting that the Gospel of Mark is not the first biblical document to create tension through references to divine hardening. The book of Exodus, from which Mark has likely learned the potential for divine hardening, also employs its hardening language so that hearers cannot ultimately discern the reason for Pharaoh's stubborn refusal to let the Israelites go. To be sure, the majority of references portray God as the explicit subject of the action, in which case God hardens Pharaoh's heart directly (Exod. 4:21; 7:3; 9:12; 10:1, 20, 27; 11:10; 14:4, 8, 17).[74] In addition to these, however, three passages explicitly state that Pharaoh actually hardens *his own* heart (8:15, 32; 9:34).[75] In the end, then, the book of Exodus creates an irresolvable tension around the issue of God and his relationship to Pharaoh. As with the Gospel of Mark, it does nothing to resolve this tension. It simply creates it, so that the audience must experience it.[76]

Finally, it is worth noting that the reality of divine hardening need not imply that Jesus and God are "working at cross purposes."[77] Once again, God continues to act invasively through Jesus and, by extension, through the disciples, even in the face of divine hardening. Apparently for Mark, then, such hardening does not run counter to Jesus' initial announcement of God's encroaching reign (1:14–15), although it does reveal certain limits in his knowledge. Along these lines one must keep in mind that setting Jesus and God at "cross-purposes" would be tantamount to setting God at odds with himself. For the conviction that God's actions in Jesus constitute "good news" underlies the entire story (1:1, 14–15); and it would be self-defeating for Mark, or any other New Testament writer, to support such a claim through the depiction of a self-contradicting God. As Jesus' early parables make clear (4:1–34), the entire story moves toward the consummation of God's reign: God will complete what God has started. Though this completion occurs outside the limits of the narrative, it hardly diminishes Jesus' assurance that God will stay true to God's word.

In this respect, then, the audience will expect God's hardening of the disciples to function in accordance with the overarching theme of divine fidelity rather than as a divinely instigated (and therefore capricious) threat to that fidelity. Though the precise reasons are yet unknown—and are never stated with certainty—hardening, the believing audience must assume, falls within the divine plan that Mark names "the good news of Jesus Christ" (1:1). God does not undermine God's own promises. In fulfilling those promises, however, God does defy human expectation. Hardening accentuates the divine mystery.

4

God Scandalizes Disciples
(8:22–15:39)

Christ, it seemed to me, was the victim of humanity's lack of imagination . . . hammered to the cross with the nails of creative vapidity.
—*Nick Cave*[1]

He began to teach them that it was necessary for the Son of Man to suffer greatly.
—*Mark 8:31*

As scholars have long noted, the midway point of the Gospel marks a clear turning point. For it is here that Mark introduces the "necessity" of Jesus' death (δεῖ, 8:31). Consequently, the narrative's focus on Jesus' miraculous ministry and its confounding effects on the disciples shifts, generally speaking, toward a focus on Jesus' opposition to the leaders (which leads ultimately to his death) and his teaching of the disciples (who refuse to accept that death as a model for their own ministry). This is not to say, however, that the encroachment of God's eschatological reign no longer factors into the audience's experience of the Gospel. Rather, the audience simply moves from an experience of God's invasive action, in its initial stages, to an experience of its hostile consequences. Stated simply, the transformative effects of God's reign meet resistance, ironically, from the very people who deem themselves God's representatives.

In this sense the British musician Nick Cave is right to characterize Mark's Jesus as "the victim of humanity's lack of imagination . . . hammered to the cross with the nails of creative vapidity." For just as the leaders cannot fathom divine inspiration in a person challenging the very laws they uphold, so the disciples cannot fathom a Messiah whose divine mission ends upon a Roman cross. Moreover, the narrative depicts a striking relationship between the responses of both groups, since the final expression of opposition from Jesus' enemies produces the final expression of opposition from his followers. In other words, Jesus' arrest triggers abandonment (14:49–50). This is what I call the "invasion logic" of Mark's passion account, according to which the "necessity" of Jesus' death stems from a divine initiative that, in turn, produces a kind of inevitable unfolding of earthly responses: God invades the world through Jesus, the threatened establishment resolves to stop that invasion, and the disciples, upon Jesus' arrest, abandon Jesus to the cross.[2]

Yet this again is only half the story, since the narrative continues to reinforce the tension of God's divergent modes of action. Thus alongside Mark's invasion logic one finds an equally compelling transcendent logic, according to which the necessity of Jesus' death stems from God's own will as anticipated by Scripture. In particular, the audience discovers that the destruction and vindication of Jesus as God's emissary (Isa. 5:1–7; Ps. 118:22–23), the desertion of Jesus' disciples (Zech. 13:7), and even the crucifixion itself (Ps. 22:1, 7, 18) stem from ancient promises that reach fulfillment in the narrative. Even Jesus' predictions about the destruction of the temple (Mark 13:1–8, 14) and the persecution of his disciples (13:9–13), though existing beyond the narrative, factor into the end times as ordained by God. Quite mysteriously, all of these events function as expressions of God's own faithfulness.

By the time Jesus has breathed his last breath, then, hearers have experienced his suffering as an irresolvable tension corresponding with the Gospel's depiction of God. Once again Mark's depiction of God bears directly upon his depiction of the disciples. For the tension surrounding God's divergent modes of action provides the audience with two equally divergent explanations for the disciples' eventual rejection of the crucified Messiah. On the one hand, God scandalizes the disciples insofar as God's invasive action elicits dangerously violent responses from the leaders, responses that repel the disciples to the point of abandoning Jesus. On the other hand, however, God scandalizes the disciples insofar as God himself wills the death of Jesus and, consequently, the abandonment of his disciples as well (14:26–31). In this sense the divine will for Jesus' death effectively replaces the motif of divine hardening (6:52; 8:17) as the primary point of contact between the disciples and God's transcendent mode of action.[3] God has in fact "scripted" them into the story of a crucified Messiah (14:21, 27).

In charting the audience's journey toward this climactic theological tension, in the present chapter I treat 8:22–15:47 in two sections. The first section, which covers 8:22–10:52, examines the way in which God scandalizes the disciples by the mere *promise* of Jesus' suffering and death. Before it is even realized, Jesus' passion challenges the disciples' imaginations to such a scandalous degree that it prohibits true understanding, thus deepening the rift between the Messiah and his followers. The second section, which covers 11:1–15:39, examines the way in which God scandalizes the disciples through the *realization* of Jesus' passion. The inevitability of this realization becomes clear as Jesus intensifies his antagonism toward the leaders (11:1–12:44); and although Mark takes care to include a hopeful window into the disciples' future (13:9–13), his depiction of Jesus' final hours (14:1–15:39) brings God's transcendent will to the surface, creating a climactic theological tension in which the disciples are directly implicated.

SCANDALIZED BY THE PROMISE OF THE CROSS (8:22–10:52)

Initial Resistance to a Crucified Messiah (8:22–33)

Although hearers already know of a plot to destroy Jesus (3:6), Jesus' own awareness (and acceptance) of his death does not fully surface until the midpoint of the narrative, during a private conversation with his disciples on the way to Caesarea Philippi (8:27–33).[4] To fully appreciate this scene, however, it helps to note the significance of its location in the larger narrative. As discussed in the previous chapter, the audience has just heard Jesus' harsh reprimand of the disciples, who have misunderstood his second miraculous feeding (8:17–21). Yet before moving to the conversation in Caesarea Philippi, Mark relates an interesting account of Jesus healing a blind man (8:22–26). The story is particularly significant in that Jesus' initial attempt at healing, contrary to narrative precedents, produces only partial results. After Jesus places saliva on the man's eyes, he exclaims, "I see people, but I perceive them as trees walking" (8:24). It is only after a second attempt, when Jesus places his hands directly upon the man's eyes, that he "sees through" (διέβλεψεν, 8:25) his blindness, regaining full sight.[5]

At one very important level this episode continues the extension of God's reign through Jesus' shalom-making ministry. At this particular stage of its narrative journey, however, an audience experiences this uniquely two-staged miracle in the context of the disciples' persistent misunderstanding, which Jesus himself has even likened to blindness (8:18). Heard in this way, the healing of the blind man represents more than a solitary episode in Jesus' ministry. It also signifies the magnitude of the spiritual blindness exhibited by his own followers, a blindness even Jesus cannot heal immediately. Moreover, it anticipates the conversation in Caesarea Philippi in which Peter recognizes Jesus as the "Christ" but, out of opposition to his impending passion, nonetheless "sees Jesus indistinctly."[6]

That conversation begins innocently enough, as Jesus poses the question to his disciples: "Who do people (οἳ ἄνθρωποι) say that I am?" (8:27). It seems that the disciples, for once in the narrative, have a question they can easily answer: "John the Baptist, and others, Elijah, and still others, one of the prophets" (8:28). When Jesus rephrases the question—"Who do *you* [plural ὑμεῖς] say that I am?" (8:29)—Peter's response serves to highlight, however fleetingly, the disciples' insider status vis-à-vis "the people." Apparently speaking on behalf of his cohorts, he correctly identifies Jesus: "You are the Christ" (8:29). Jesus then orders them all to keep silent about his identity, thus implying his agreement with Peter's claim (8:30).

Peter's identification of Jesus is not only correct. It is also somewhat puzzling, at least for the audience that appreciates the irony of Mark's discourse and understands the ramifications of the claim. For up to this point in the narrative the word "Christ" (χριστός) has appeared only once, in the very first verse (1:1), and in a direct communication from Mark to his audience. In other words, while Jesus' status as Christ has been a fundamental part of Mark's discourse, it has not been a part of Jesus' teaching in the narrative. Only the audience has had access to this knowledge. Thus Peter's "confession," as it is so often called, comes somewhat as a surprise.[7] Indeed, due to this moment of unexpected clarity, one is tempted to view this conversation as a secondary climax to the Gospel as a whole. After so much misunderstanding, here the disciples finally get something right!

But the conversation is hardly over. If this episode functions as a secondary climax it is not because of Peter's insight into Jesus' identity. Rather, it is because of the momentous resistance to Jesus that the conversation quickly elicits, a resistance so severely condemned by Jesus that the audience must question the extent to which Peter really understands his master at all. This resistance comes as a response to Jesus' first passion prediction, which Jesus gives immediately after swearing the disciples to silence: "He began to teach them that it was necessary (δεῖ) for the Son of Man to suffer greatly, be rejected by the elders and chief priests and scribes, be killed, and after three days rise again" (8:31). It is the first explicit mention of Jesus' death that the disciples have heard.

Caught off guard, Peter responds to Jesus' prediction (presumably on behalf of the group again) by "rebuking" him (ἐπιτιμάω, 8:32), a rather astonishing action given its forceful connotation in the context of Jesus' exorcisms (1:25; 4:39; 9:25). Jesus, for his part, responds with a "rebuke" of his own (8:33), reinforcing the exorcism motif in a most startling way: "Get behind me, Satan! For you are not setting your mind on the things of God but on the things of humans" (8:33). In thinking "the things of humans" (τὰ τῶν ἀνθρώπων), Peter becomes (or simply is) a *satan*, or "adversary," of the very one he purports to follow. Such human things, manifested in Peter's rebuke, stand dia-metrically opposed to "the things of God" manifested in Jesus' future as cru-cified Messiah.[8]

Clearly at the heart of this disagreement is the question of how one under-stands the word "Christ," or "anointed one" (*messiah*, as it is often transliter-ated from the Hebrew). Indeed, based on the history of the word's meaning, Peter seems to have a valid point in the debate, or at least a perspective with which hearers may empathize. For although it is clear that ancient Jews, as an enormously diverse group of people, "did not profess a coherent and norma-tive messianology,"[9] it is equally clear that their thoughts on the subject "did not allow for a *crucified* 'Messiah.'"[10] To be God's end-time Anointed logically precluded suffering and death. Thus Mark's depiction of the confrontation between Jesus and Peter symbolizes, in many respects, the manner in which the early church introduced a theological *novum* into its own Jewish world-view.[11] More to the point, it provides a clear instance of historical realism, par-ticularly in Peter's harsh reaction to Jesus' prediction. Thus, even though he does not reveal his particular messianic expectations, "we can forgive Peter if all of Jesus' new talk about suffering, rejection, and death does not sound right to him."[12]

Though a strictly historical investigation yields only diverse (and often-times conflicting) messianic expectations, one can rather easily discern the kinds of messianic expectations that concern this particular narrator. Espe-cially when one looks ahead to the actual passion account, it is clear that Mark understands the term "Christ" as a *royal* designation. Pontius Pilate and the Roman soldiers mock Jesus as "King of the Jews" (15:2, 9, 12, 16–20); the plac-ard hanging upon his cross says the same (15:26); and the chief priests and scribes, no doubt savoring Jesus' execution, sarcastically exclaim: "Let the Messiah, the King of Israel, now come down from the cross, in order that we may see and believe" (15:32; cf. 4:12). When coupled with Mark's use of a royal psalm to designate Jesus' status as "Son of God" (1:11; Ps. 2:7),[13] these refer-ences indicate that, for Mark at least, calling Jesus the Christ/Anointed is tan-tamount to calling him God's *king*, with the result that his crucifixion necessarily invites ridicule and scorn.[14] Kings are supposed to wield power, not fall victim to it.

The irony of Mark's passion account lies not only in the ridicule, torture, and crucifixion of Jesus as God's alleged king. Equally ironic, and more fun-damental to Mark's portrait of Jesus, is that those who mock him actually speak the truth. For Jesus—at least from the perspective of God, Mark, and the audi-ence—is in fact the very king he is mocked as. "The irony in the story is pro-nounced," Juel notes, "but it only works if Jesus is the Christ—and if the religious and political leaders speak for the tradition and common sense."[15] To fully appreciate Mark's story, then, one must recognize both sides of this equation, that Jesus is indeed the Christ and that his opponents mock him based on "tradition and common sense," that is, from a perspective that does not have access to Mark's discourse. Viewed from the perspective "of humans," as Jesus calls it, the Messiah *by definition* does not suffer. Thus bystanders to the crucifixion know Jesus to be a false Messiah precisely because he hangs upon a Roman cross. From the perspective of Mark's discourse, however, the audience sees that bystanders have in effect been blinded by the very reality they behold. Their imaginations do not encompass Mark's own theological alternative. They have eyes to see but do not see.

Although the blinding effect of a crucified Messiah is perhaps most pronounced among Jesus' executioners and enemies, it first surfaces on the way to Caesarea Philippi, among Jesus' closest followers. Along these lines it is crucial to note that 8:21–33 focuses less on the rationale behind Peter's clairvoyant "confession" than on his hostile response to Jesus' passion prediction, a response that elicits a rather elaborate teaching moment from Jesus (8:34–9:1). Thus, for whatever reason, Peter gets the words right ("You are the Christ"); yet he clearly makes this assertion from the perspective "of humans," thus implying that he does not understand Jesus' identity at all. Based on the severity of his reaction (a confrontational "rebuke"), this seems the reason Peter cannot stand for Jesus' morbidly bold prediction: the human imagination simply excludes suffering and death as a possibility for God's Anointed. Such a scenario is truly absurd, as if one were to say, for instance, that by losing one's life one could save it (8:35). In this way Peter does not simply disagree with Jesus, as if it were simply a matter of opinion. Like the bystanders at Golgotha, he *knows* his master to be wrong.[16]

Divine Necessity, Continued Resistance (8:33–10:52)

Yet even this explanation does not fully capture the irony of Peter's misunderstanding, since it fails to account for God's role in Jesus' violent future. Indeed, as Johnson has remarked, 8:31–33 is "more about who God is than who Jesus is or whether or not Peter's confession in 8:29 is inaccurate, wrongheaded, or right but inadequate."[17] Stated simply, the revelation of the Christ's passion is ultimately a statement about the God whose reign Jesus brings. For in opposing Jesus' promised passion Peter actually, though unknowingly, opposes the divine will. The first clue to this comes in the language of the promise itself: "He began to teach them that *it was necessary* for the Son of Man to suffer greatly."[18] The Greek term used to designate necessity (δεῖ) will reappear in conjunction with the coming of Elijah (9:11), the future tribulation (13:7, 14), and the disciples' promised ministry "to all the nations" (13:10). As the audience proceeds along its narrative journey, then, it will come to associate the term with divinely ordained end-time events, thus reinforcing the sense in which Jesus' first passion prediction suggests the same.[19]

More forceful than this subtle clue, however, is that Jesus reprimands the disciples[20] by drawing a stark contrast between "the things of God" and "the things of humans" (8:33). If the disciples' opposition to the divine will was not yet clear to the audience, here it becomes obvious. Indeed, so strongly do "the things of humans" contradict "the things of God" (at least on this particular issue) that Jesus can call Peter, the first and most outspoken disciple, an outright "adversary" ("satan," σατανᾶς). This casts Jesus' followers in a light alarmingly similar to the leaders. Of course in the case of the disciples such opposition is directed toward Jesus' death (not his actual ministry and messianic claims), and results in only a brief rebuke (not extensive ridicule and conspiracy). With respect to both groups, however, the audience finds adversaries whose rejection of Jesus stems ultimately from the limits of the imagination— the imagination constrained by "the things of humans."[21] Although the actual point of contention has shifted from earlier chapters, then, the disciples still seem not to understand the one they follow.

It is worth noting that this is not the first time the audience has heard Jesus distinguish between divine and human perspectives. The distinction first arose in a debate in which Jesus criticized the scribes and Pharisees for their unnecessarily strict purity laws:

> He said to them, "Isaiah prophesied rightly about you hypocrites, as it is written, 'This people honors me with their lips, but their hearts are far from me; they worship me in vain, teaching doctrines as *human commandments*.' Dismissing the *commandment of God*, you hold fast to *the tradition of humans*." Then he said to them, "How well you reject the *commandment of God* in order to uphold your tradition!" (7:6–9).

This scathing critique introduces the famous speech in which Jesus, according to Mark's account, declares "all foods clean" (7:19). For present purposes, however, more significant is Mark's introduction of the diametrical opposition between the human and divine perspective. Mark drives this distinction home with noticeable repetition (as shown in the above quotation), placing the scribes and Pharisees in a position of direct antagonism to God, who here accosts them through the Scriptures (Isa. 7:6–7).[22] When, therefore, the audience finds itself along the road to Caesarea Philippi, the sharp distinction drawn by Jesus at Mark 8:33 carries added significance. The disciples' alignment with "the things of humans," over against "the things of God," places them in poor company indeed. More to the point, it reinforces the extent to which their opposition to Jesus' passion, originating in their limited human perspective, sets them against the divine will.

The newly announced connection between the divine will and the passion of Jesus adds a profound theological dimension to the audience's experience of the Gospel. It should be noted, however, that the precise relationship between God and the cross is not altogether clear. The language of necessity (δεῖ), coupled with the strong distinction between divine and human perspectives, suggests for the first time in the narrative that God wills the death of Jesus. This raises the possibility, also for the first time in the narrative, that the passion is somehow divinely foreordained (what I have called Mark's transcendent logic of the cross).[23] That possibility is confirmed soon after Jesus' transfiguration, when he boldly connects his passion to the Scriptures: "How is it written (γέγραπται) about the Son of Man, that he is to suffer many things and be rejected?" (9:12).

Previous to the conversation in Caesarea Philippi, however, the narrative strongly suggested that the leaders' antagonism toward Jesus stemmed directly from Jesus' own ministry, in which case one might just as easily interpret the passion's necessity as an inevitable outcome. According to this invasive logic, the cross is necessary to the extent that Jesus' ministry is necessary, and Jesus' ministry necessarily results in death because of the hostility it inevitably elicits from powerful people. God "wills" Jesus' death, in this case, only insofar as God wills to exercise his eschatological reign through Jesus, and only insofar as Jesus, possessed by God's Spirit, refuses to relinquish his authority in bringing that reign.[24]

In both cases, Jesus clearly faces an uphill battle as he begins to teach the disciples about the significance of his passion for the task of discipleship (8:34–9:1). As if looking for anyone with ears to hear, he even calls the surrounding crowd to attention: "If anyone (τις) wishes to follow me let them deny themselves, take up their cross, and follow me. For whoever (ὅς) wishes to save his life will lose it, and whoever (ὅς) wishes to lose his life because of me and the gospel will save it" (8:34–35). The reference to "following behind me" (ὀπίσω μου ἀκολουθεῖν), while serving as a kind of invitation at one level, also takes the audience back to the lakeshore of Galilee, when the fishermen were first summoned to their eschatological vocation (1:16–20). This suggests that Jesus intends not simply to find more followers (which does not appear to happen anyway) but, more importantly, to clarify the consequences of following for those having already joined him along the "way" (ὁδός, 1:2, 3; 6:8; 8:27; 9:33–34; 10:17, 32, 52).[25] To truly follow the Messiah who "must" die means placing oneself on the path of suffering and death, that is, serving others "even if such service provokes a response from the powerful that leads to suffering and/or death."[26] It means losing one's own life and, paradoxically through that loss, saving it.

The confusion on the way to Caesarea Philippi is only the beginning. For as scholars have long noted, 8:27–9:1 forms only the first of three nearly successive episodes modeled on the same basic pattern: a passion prediction (8:31–32a; 9:30–32; 10:32–34), followed by an instance of the disciples' misunderstanding (8:32b–33; 9:33–34; 10:35–40), followed by a teaching on discipleship (8:34–9:1; 9:35–37; 10:41–45).[27] In every case the misunderstanding of the disciples suggests their collective resistance to the promise of Jesus' suffering, as well as their contrasting hopes for a triumphant and glorious future. Conversely, Jesus' teachings counter such priorities by lifting up his passion as a model for the disciples' ministry. That is, while the disciples envision their vocation on the traditional model of a power-wielding Christ, Jesus insists that the Christ "came not to be served but to serve" (10:45).

The threefold repetition of this pattern clarifies some things while complicating others. It clarifies that the disciples do not resist Jesus' passion out of some altruistic concern for his well-being but rather because it conflicts with their own self-serving ambitions.[28] It also illustrates Jesus' persistent desire for the disciples to overcome such worldly priorities, to embrace the necessity of his passion, and to model its self-giving logic themselves. Along these lines 8:27–10:45 encourages the audience to follow Jesus' lead in holding the disciples accountable for their misunderstanding, for Jesus presumably would not explain things to the disciples if they were not, in his view at least, capable of understanding him. Although hearers may empathize with Peter's opposition to Jesus' first passion prediction, then, such empathy slowly turns to frustration with each subsequent misunderstanding. The dynamic here closely parallels that of Jesus' miracles, and especially his two feeding miracles, in which the disciples failed to understand despite multiple opportunities.

Having experienced that earlier confusion over miracles, however, the audience also knows that Jesus' immediate intentions for the disciples may not necessarily align with the action of God in the story, for in the former case the disciples' confusion was equally attributable to both obstinacy and divine hardening. For that reason the threefold cycle of 8:27–10:45 raises questions about the precise nature of the disciples' resistance. This is underscored by the fact that Mark situates the second and third cycles of misunderstanding after the transfiguration (9:1–8), a scene in which *God* directly instructs Peter, James, and John to heed Jesus' words (9:7).[29] Yet they still fail to do so. Thus it becomes increasingly more difficult to tell whether the disciples' resistance to the passion stems from obstinacy or outright inability. In other words, do the disciples dwell on "the things of humans" because they are simply self-serving, or because they are simply human? Is their blindness to the passion's necessity self-imposed and thus curable by mere teaching, or is the necessity itself so blinding that something more than teaching, however repetitive, is required?[30]

Mark's answer is a paradoxical yes. As in earlier chapters, the narrative supports divergent explanations for the disciples' misunderstanding. So although the point of contention may have shifted—from the significance of Jesus' miracles to the necessity of his passion—the basic dynamic remains the same: the disciples are, and are not, able to understand Jesus. Yet the new point of contention is highly significant theologically, for Mark attributes the necessity of Jesus' passion to God's own divergent actions. So it is not simply a question of misunderstanding but, more specifically, a question of misunderstanding the divine will. Along these lines, Mark is equally ambiguous about *what* exactly the disciples misunderstand about God. Do they fail to accept that Jesus' ministry will inevitably result in death (a matter of God's invasive activity)? Or do they fail to accept that God has foreordained Jesus to die (a matter of God's transcendent activity)? Here too the ambiguity of the Gospel implies a paradoxical yes.

Having created so much tension over the question of the disciples' misunderstanding, Mark concludes the threefold cycle with a more assuring story about the healing of a second blind man, Bartimaeus (10:46–52). As with the first blind man (8:22–26), the healing here does more than reinforce Jesus' miraculous power to cure physical infirmity. It also speaks to Jesus' power to cure the spiritual blindness of his own disciples. In this case, however, the healing is immediate (not two-staged) and elicits a disciple like act from the one healed: Bartimaeus "follows" Jesus "on the way" to Jerusalem (10:52). The placing of this episode after so much misunderstanding could not be timelier, as it suggests to hearers that blindness will not last forever, and that the healing of blindness, whenever it comes, frees people to follow Jesus.[31] Although such reassurance does not resolve the Gospel's present tension, it does point to a time beyond it.

SCANDALIZED BY THE REALITY OF THE CROSS (11:1–15:39)

Intensification of Conflict in Jerusalem (11:1–12:44)

The audience knows from Jesus' third passion prediction that he will die in Jerusalem, and that the leaders there (chief priests and scribes) will be the ones to "condemn him to death and hand him over to the Gentiles" (10:32–34). It is significant, then, that Mark moves quickly from the threefold cycle of prediction/misunderstanding/teaching to Jesus' arrival in Jerusalem and the intensification of conflict with the temple establishment.[32] This prevents any significant lapse in narrative time between the promises of Jesus' passion, on the one hand, and the fulfillment of those promises on the other hand. Thus the life-giving mode of discipleship just described by Jesus (8:34–38; 9:33–37;

10:41–45) will soon find its origins in Jesus' own death, making him the first to realize his own teachings while also validating, once and for all, his prophetic reliability.[33] As for the disciples themselves, however, Jesus' arrival in Jerusalem marks their temporary withdrawal to the background of the narrative. For this reason, I will not concentrate heavily upon 11:1–12:44 except to discuss the way in which this section develops the theological tension of the passion, particularly as it is expressed in Jesus' condemnatory parable against the temple establishment at 12:1–12.

Hearers experience the invasive side of this tension in the narrative buildup to the parable. Jesus enters the temple and enacts a symbolic demonstration against it (11:15–17), a demonstration most likely stemming from the socially unjust practices of the temple's own caretakers (11:17; 12:38–44).[34] In this way the subsequent hostility to Jesus stems from Jesus' own initiative in the story. He does not wander aimlessly into the temple and decide, out of some unspoken impulse, to condemn its administrators. On the contrary, Jesus' ominous first appearance in the temple on the previous day (11:11), along with the scriptural background of his prophetic speech (Isa. 56:7; Jer. 7:11), suggests that the temple has been his intended destination. The intercalation of his condemnation with the cursing of the fig tree (11:12–14, 20–26) confirms this intention, indicating that Jesus does not act impulsively but by prophetic commission. Thus the very place in which God was believed to dwell now stands condemned by God's own Messiah.[35]

Remaining consistent with the pattern of earlier conflicts (2:1–3:6; 3:20–30), Mark also depicts the leaders' antagonistic response to Jesus. The chief priests, scribes, and elders demand from him an explanation for his seemingly irreverent actions: "By what authority are you doing these things? Who gave you the authority to do them?" (11:28). Though the immediate narrative context places these questions alongside Jesus' temple condemnation, the audience knows the issue of Jesus' authority (ἐξουσία) has fueled his conflict with the leaders from the very beginning (1:22, 27; 2:10). Jesus' counterquestions (11:29–30) reframe the debate around the authority of John the Baptist, a move that seems to bewilder the leaders but again strikes the audience as appropriate, since the same divine authority underlies the ministries of both men. So even though the leaders evade Jesus' questions by refusing to answer, Mark's hearers have nonetheless been reminded of the underlying theological dimensions of the conflict. The caretakers of God's house stand, unknowingly, in the course of God's encroaching reign and, by virtue of their opposition to that reign, stand condemned by their own God.

It is here that Jesus, filling the leaders' awkward silence, offers his equally condemnatory parable of the Tenants (12:1–12), a parable that not only clarifies the basic plot of the story (much like the parables of 4:1–34) but also reinforces the

Gospel's theological tension from both sides. Here, however, the tension pertains specifically to the violent fate of God's "beloved" Son (12:6; cf. 1:11; 9:7),
who, having been sent by God to collect "the fruit of the vineyard" (12:2),
meets rejection and death at the hands of tenants, the very ones to whom God
has entrusted his property. For Mark's hearers the parable's basic allegorical
significance is clear: coming at the end of a long history of rejected prophets
(12:2–5), Jesus represents God's final move to reclaim what belongs to him.
The owner's final destruction of the tenants, and the handing over of the
vineyards to "others" (12:9), anticipates the downfall of the corrupt temple
establishment (13:1–2), as well as God's incorporation of those outside the
establishment's traditional purview.[36]

In this way Jesus really does answer, albeit in parabolic form, the leaders'
question about his authority. The parable asserts that Jesus condemns the temple not as some crazed lunatic, lacking the proper authority, but rather as God's
ultimate emissary, the beloved Son. Hearers will recall that Jesus' status as
beloved Son was revealed by means of his unique possession by God (1:11),
which also makes him the agent of God's eschatological reign. Soon to become
"the stone that the builders rejected" this beloved Son will be vindicated, by
virtue of God's "amazing" plan, into "the cornerstone" itself (12:10–11). Indeed,
by the time Jesus has finished speaking, Mark's audience understands the parable primarily as a story about God, "the only character who remains from the
beginning to the end."[37] It is God who plants the vineyard, God who owns its
produce, and God who takes action to reclaim both.

Mark makes clear that the parable does not confound the leaders entirely.
They recognize that it is spoken "against them" and begin looking for an
opportunity to arrest Jesus (12:12), thus continuing the gradual fulfillment of
previous passion predictions. The full significance of the parable resonates primarily with Mark's hearers, however, not only because it confirms their understanding of Jesus' identity but also because it intensifies their experience of the
Gospel's underlying theological tension, now with respect to Jesus' impending death. Particularly with respect to God's invasive action, the parable reinforces the dynamic begun in earlier chapters (2:1–3:6; 3:20–30; 7:1–24)
whereby leaders oppose the action of God in their midst. Viewed from this
angle, the death of the beloved Son stems from the volition of the tenants in
hostile and selfish response to the vineyard owner's actions (12:7–8). At the
same time, however, the parable's strong indebtedness to Scripture raises the
possibility of God's transcendent action, for Jesus has already mentioned how
his passion will unfold "as it is written" (9:12). Hearing that same passion now
described with strong references to Isa. 5:1–7, coupled with a direct quotation
of Ps. 118:22–23, the audience now returns to the question of how exactly to

interpret the divine necessity of Jesus' death: Do the Scriptures merely predict the way events will unfold, or does the unfolding itself reveal the will of God?

Although the former possibility brings a tidy coherence to the narrative, the latter cannot be dismissed outright. In his quotation of Psalm 118, for instance, Jesus does not clarify what exactly is "the Lord's doing" that is "amazing in our eyes" (12:11). Is it strictly the vindication of the stone after its rejection, or is it both the vindication and the rejection? Moreover, is there significance in that the term used for rejection (ἀποδοκιμάζειν, 12:10) echoes Jesus' first passion prediction (8:31), which grounded that rejection in divine necessity (δεῖ, 8:31) and "the things of God" (8:33)?[38] Due to Mark's ambiguity, the audience's sense of God's transcendent action is perhaps less acute than its sense of God's invasive action. Nonetheless, the sheer possibility of God's transcendent action, first raised in chapter 8, brings an element of tension to its experience of the parable.

This emerging tension adds an element of mystery to the flurry of confrontations that immediately follow: the debates over Roman taxation (12:13–17), resurrection from the dead (12:18–27), and the Messiah's Davidic lineage (12:35–37). Hearers must now ask: Is this intensification of conflict a matter of earthly resistance to God's eschatological invasion, or is the conflict itself a part of God's own will for the Messiah? True to form, the Gospel has begun to supply both explanations, and it will gradually reinforce the tension as it brings the reality of God's transcendent action more noticeably to the surface, particularly through repeated allusions to Scripture. It will not be long until the audience again hears Jesus refer to his own fate in terms of scriptural "fulfillment" (14:49; cf. 9:12).

Meanwhile, it is worth noting that Jesus' parable has created a subtle incongruence between what literary critics commonly call the first and second "degrees" of the narrative.[39] At the level of second-degree narrative (the story within the story), the parable portrays the tenants of God's vineyard as entirely conscious of the Son's identity; and it is their recognition of the Son that motivates their rejection of him: "This is the heir. Come, let us kill him, and the inheritance will be ours" (12:7). At the level of first-degree narrative (the larger Gospel story), however, Jesus' opponents (represented in the parable by the tenants) exhibit no such consciousness. Indeed, their rejection of Jesus stems precisely from their *failure* to recognize him as the beloved Son; and this failure stems in turn from their refusal to identify with the wicked tenants in the parable. They grasp the basic logic of the parable (12:12) but resist its application. "Yes we are God's tenants," they seem to say, "but we are not *those* tenants, and you are certainly not God's beloved Son. Instead, we are protecting God's house from the likes of you." From their perspective, it is unimaginable for God to threaten the very ones entrusted to care for God's house.

Given this incongruence it would be wrong, in my view, to read the parable of 12:1–12 as a kind of psychological commentary on the leaders' opposition to Jesus. Generally speaking, however, it does clarify the sense of entitlement underlying that opposition, so that the leaders prove to be protectors of power and self-interest rather than servants of the divine will ("Is it not written, 'My house shall be called a house of prayer for all the nations'? But you have made it a den of robbers!" 11:17). This, of course, was essentially the same dynamic at work in Jesus' early confrontations in Galilee, in which he attacked the leaders' conservative approach to Torah and its consequent marginalization of the needy. It was also the underlying focus of (or foil in) his teachings on discipleship, which attempted to dissuade his followers from an infatuation with power and place them squarely on "the way" of a crucified Messiah.

It is appropriate, then, that Mark concludes this series of confrontations by bringing the disciples back onto the narrative stage. "Beware of the scribes," Jesus warns them, for they like "to walk in robes, to be saluted in the marketplaces, to have the best seats in the synagogues and places of honor at meals" (12:38–39). At one level this teaching functions simply as a call to recognition: take note of how not to act (cf. 10:35–45), and instead look to the poor widow who, in the gift of two small coins, gives "her whole life" to the temple treasury (12:41–44). Yet there is also an element of real warning, for it is presumably gifts like the widow's that fund the extravagance of the temple scribes (so 12:40). Thus the widow is not simply a foil but a victim.[40] Consequently, Jesus has clarified not only the difference between true and false piety but, more fundamentally, the potential for falsely pious people to take the lives of God's true servants. As the audience will soon learn, the command to "beware" (Βλέπετε, 12:38) implies not only an ethical imperative but a promise of imminent danger.

Eschatological Promises (13:1–37)

It is with the very next scene, during Jesus' lengthy eschatological speech (13:1–37), that Mark confirms the promissory dimension of the command to "beware" (Βλέπετε, 13:5, 9, 23, 33). Speaking in response to the disciples' awed admiration for the temple (13:1), Jesus prophesies a whole litany of events (both human and cosmic), culminating in the glorious and powerful coming of the Son of Man "to gather his elect from the four winds" (13:27). Between warnings about the temple's destruction (13:1–8) and the final tribulations (13:4–23), Jesus makes the following prediction about the disciples:

> As for yourselves, beware (Βλέπετε); for they will hand you over (παραδώσουσιν ὑμᾶς) to councils; and you will be beaten in synagogues; and you will stand before governors and kings because of me (ἕνεκεν ἐμοῦ), as a testimony to them. And the good news must first

be proclaimed (δεῖ κηρυχθῆναι τὸ εὐαγγέλιον) to all nations. When they bring you to trial and hand you over (ὑμᾶς παραδιδόντες), do not worry beforehand about what you are to say; but say whatever is given you (δοθῇ ὑμῖν) at that time, for it is not you who speak, but the Holy Spirit. Brother will betray brother to death, and a father his child, and children will rise against parents and have them put to death; and you will be hated by all because of my name (διὰ τὸ ὄνομά μου). But the one who endures to the end will be delivered (13:9–13).

With these words Mark assures his audience of the disciples' future role within the unfolding plan of God. It is an assurance the audience needs since the disciples have fared rather poorly over the course of the narrative, particularly since the quarrel on the way to Caesarea Philippi (8:27–33). Given this momentum, one may very easily begin to question whether the disciples will again realize their vocation as fishers of people. Jesus here dismisses such doubts, however, promising that the disciples will give their whole lives to their eschatological task and will thus come to exemplify Jesus' previous teachings. As with the parables of chapter 4, Jesus gives hope in the face of troubling circumstances.

The promise of true discipleship also includes unmistakable theological undertones. To begin, the narrative context of the passage—an extensive prophecy about the end times drawing repeatedly from the book of Daniel[41]—implies that such discipleship will emerge as a result of the unfolding of God's will. In this way Mark's use of the future tense functions reassuringly—again, as an expression of hope—and not merely to distinguish events temporally. More specifically, the passage reiterates the divine necessity (δεῖ, 13:10) expressed in Jesus' first passion prediction (8:31), giving the audience as much certainty about the disciples' proclamation of the gospel to the nations as it has about Jesus' impending death. Finally, that the disciples will be *given* words to say (passive δοθῇ, 13:11) implies the activity of God, an activity made explicit in the subsequent reference to the Holy Spirit, which, according to Jesus, will bear witness before worldly powers through the disciples (13:11).

In placing the disciples' future within the unfolding plan of God, Mark also makes sure to express, once again, the affinities between their eschatological vocation and Jesus' own ministry. Mark first drew these parallels with the appointing (3:7–19) and commissioning (6:7–13, 30–32) of the Twelve, so that the audience came to see the disciples as extensions (or at least potential extensions) of Jesus' ministry in the world. In a similar vein, Mark here describes the disciples' future in direct parallel to Jesus' ministry, though here the affinities pertain primarily to Jesus' coming passion. Like Jesus, they will be handed over (13:9, 11; cf. 3:19; 14:10, 11) to councils (13:9; cf. 14:55; 15:1), where they will be beaten (13:9; cf. 12:3, 5; 14:65; 15:15) by earthly rulers and required to testify before them (13:9, 11; cf. 14:53–65; 15:1–5). Thus they will exemplify the teachings they have heretofore resisted.

In keeping with earlier chapters, Mark keeps this positive glimpse on the disciples short, thus maintaining the tension between present circumstances (the disciples' misunderstanding) and future hope (God's fishers). In a development from earlier chapters, however, the future now promises suffering as well. Following the logic of Jesus' speech, this suffering, which takes the crucified Messiah as its model, factors into the initial encroachment of God's reign prior to its consummation with the coming Son of Man. It is not the audience's "final hope" but rather an intermediate hope marking the full realization of Jesus' initial promise to the disciples (1:17). Much like the healing of blind Bartimaeus, it is a promise that vision will be granted, and that the healed will follow the way of discipleship.

Such a promise resonates deeply for a believing audience that already considers itself a community of disciples. First, Mark's Jesus has already shown a tendency to project his teachings outside the narrative, particularly through appeals to "anyone" and "whoever."[42] So also in this case, Jesus concludes his speech by widening his projected audience from "you" to "all" (13:37).[43] Moreover, Jesus addresses events beyond the limits of the narrative, that is, events roughly contemporary with the audience. This is the case even for hearers experiencing the Gospel after, for instance, the destruction of the temple (13:2), since those same hearers still live prior to the coming Son of Man (13:26–27). In this way Mark blurs the distinction between disciples inside and outside the narrative, thereby encouraging the latter group to see itself in Jesus' promises. *All* followers of Jesus may expect not only to extend God's eschatological reign into the world but also—and as a consequence—to face violent resistance "on account of" (13:9) the one commissioning them.

In so implicating his audience, Mark heightens the sense of urgency and anticipation with respect to the end times. One might even argue that the urgency and anticipation outside the narrative surpasses that within the narrative, since hearers stand closer to the end times than the characters. Thus Jesus' exhortations to "beware" (13:9, 23, 33), "learn" (13:28), "be alert" (13:33), and "keep awake" (13:35, 37) pertain more directly to Mark's discourse than to Mark's story per se.[44] Paying close attention to these imperatives, the audience discovers that promises of future persecution (13:9–13) are accompanied by, and give rise to, promises of final glory (13:24–27). Moreover, it is precisely the trustworthiness of these promises that demands the audience's preparedness, for although the precise timetable is uncertain (13:32), the final outcome is not.[45] The Son of Man will indeed come to consummate God's reign (13:24–27). "Therefore keep awake, for you do not know when the master (ὁ κύριος) of the house is coming" (13:35).

Shepherd Struck, Sheep Scattered (14:1–15:39)

The brief window into the disciples' future at 13:9–13 stands in stark contrast to the Gospel's closing chapters, preparing the audience for what one might otherwise (i.e., in the absence of 13:9–13) construe as an utterly hopeless scenario.[46] Once Jesus enters Jerusalem, Mark significantly lessens the hurried pace of the narrative, so that the closer the Christ moves toward his necessary death, the slower and more measured the narration becomes.[47] With respect to the disciples, this deceleration in narrative pace allows Mark to depict, in rather painstaking detail, the wholesale abandonment of Jesus by his closest followers, followed by his abandonment by God (15:34).

In anticipation of that abandonment, Mark concludes Jesus' eschatological speech by mentioning how the chief priests and scribes resolve to arrest Jesus in order to destroy him (14:1). Although the audience has been aware of this intention since 12:12 (and, with respect to the Pharisees, since 3:6), here Mark specifies the means by which Jesus' opponents will seize him, namely, "by cunning" (ἐν δόλῳ, 14:1). This detail clarifies the betraying role of Judas—first mentioned at 3:19 and soon to be confirmed at 14:10–11—revealing again the alarming intersection of Mark's two major subplots. "The one who attacked the money changers and victim mongers is about to be bought as a victim himself"[48]—and sold by one of his own followers. In all of this the echo of Jesus' third passion prediction is unmistakable: "the Son of Man will be handed over to the chief priests and scribes" (10:33).

The Judas subplot encapsulates the theological tension surrounding Jesus' impending death. For on the one hand the conspiracy itself suggests Mark's invasive logic: Jesus will die as the result of the decisions and interactions of human characters, even though the precise reasons for Judas's betrayal go unmentioned.[49] Along these lines it is appropriate that during his Passover meal with the disciples Jesus expresses, "woe to that person by whom the Son of Man is handed over" (14:21b). After all, such actions ultimately oppose the encroachment of God's own reign and therefore warrant divine judgment (14:21c). Yet concerning that same betrayal Jesus claims also that "the Son of Man goes *as it is written* (καθὼς γέγραπται)" (14:21a), so that the same conspiracy also follows a divinely ordained script.[50] In a single breath, then, Jesus confirms both the invasive and transcendent logic of his passion, reinforcing the Gospel's theological tension in perhaps the most acute manner since 8:17.[51]

Nor is Judas the only disciple implicated in God's script. Jesus makes this clear after leading the disciples to the Mount of Olives (14:26). "You will all be made to stumble," he tells them, "because it is written, 'I will strike the shepherd, and the sheep will be scattered'" (14:27). The statement does not merely predict the disciples' collective involvement in Jesus' arrest—although it does do that—but also grounds that prediction in an ancient promise. More to the point, it grounds such involvement in a promise of divine action. The disciples, Jesus claims, "will be *made to stumble*" (πάντες σκανδαλισθήσεσθε). Then, as if to eliminate any speculation as to why ("because," ὅτι) he quotes Zech. 13:7: "I will strike the shepherd, and the sheep will be scattered."[52] The first-person verb (πατάξω, "*I* will strike") is a Markan modification, drawing attention to God as both the speaker and future actor (cf. 1:2–3).[53] God, then, will cause the disciples to stumble, will make them scatter—albeit indirectly through the crucifixion.

That such action is indirect does not take away from the fact that the disciples abandon Jesus "because it is written." In this sense Mark includes all of the disciples, and not just Judas, in the divine script of Jesus' passion. It should also be noted, however, that the promise of the disciples' abandonment also provides the clearest window into the transcendent logic underlying Jesus' "necessary" death (8:31). The disciples will scatter precisely because God will strike the shepherd. In boldly plain terms, then, Mark encourages the audience to experience the crucifixion itself as an act of God—not as an inevitable consequence of God's invasive action (through Jesus) but as God's transcendent action (apart from and against Jesus). Thus, in summarizing the full ramification of 14:27, Francis Moloney astutely notes that "God's design lies behind the death of Jesus, and it has the necessary consequence of the scattering of the sheep."[54]

Though hearers may sympathize with Peter's resistance to Jesus' ominous promise (14:29), they must also reckon with the divine reality now manifest in the narrative's unfolding events. Seen in this light, such resistance resembles the confrontation of 8:31–33, for Peter again speaks out against "the things of God." Although Jesus responds simply with another promise, rather than a harsh scolding (cf. 8:33), the promise nonetheless reinforces the futility of resisting God's plan: "Truly I tell you, today, on this very night, before the cock crows twice you will deny me three times" (14:30). At least in the case of Peter, abandonment will mean not only desertion but outright renunciation, an ironic twist given Jesus' previous insistence that Peter deny *himself* (8:34),[55] not to mention the promise that he will preach "to all the nations" (13:10). Again, the intermediate promise of Jesus' passion must precede the final promise of God's consummate reign. While the promise of restoration in Galilee (14:28) brings much-needed assurance (much like 13:9–13), it hardly cancels the ominous tone of the conversation.[56]

Moving the scene from the Mount of Olives to Gethsemane (14:32–42), Mark begins to set God's script into motion. Growing "disturbed and troubled" (14:33), Jesus leaves the disciples to pray in solitude, bringing only Peter, James, and John with him. Despite Jesus' repeated commands, however, the three prove unable to "stay awake" (γρηγορέω, 14:34, 37, 38).[57] Here Mark's ordering of events suggests the certainty of God's will even in spite of Jesus' own efforts. First, Jesus' prayer (14:36) raises the possibility of another course of divine action: "Abba, Father, for you all things are possible. Take from me this cup!" Then it asserts his submission to God: "Yet not what I want, but what you want." Jesus repeats this prayer three times, and each time returns to find God's immediate answer to his prayers: sleeping disciples.[58] The fact that "anything is possible" with God only accentuates the inevitability of the specific possibility God is bringing about. Jesus now stands alone before the divine will. As Tannehill notes: "Hopes for a way around the cross . . . have been aroused sufficiently to be recognized and then have been crushed."[59]

With the arrival of Judas, accompanied by a mob sent by the temple leaders (14:43), slumber quickly turns into the promised desertion (14:44–52). Here Jesus, in submitting to his arresters, echoes his own previous claim (14:21) that the betrayal of Judas follows the divine script: "in order that the scriptures might be fulfilled" (14:49; NRSV: "Let the scriptures be fulfilled"). Not surprisingly, the arrest itself also sets into motion the abandonment promised by God: "And deserting him, they all fled" (14:50). Thus as God's striking of the shepherd commences, the scattering of the sheep instantly comes to pass. This action creates an antithesis to 3:13–19, a scene in which Jesus, in response to growing hostility toward his ministry (3:6), appoints the Twelve "in order that they might be with him" (3:14).

The magnitude of this abandonment Mark captures by elaborating on the fate of two disciples in particular. First, and more briefly, an unnamed follower proves so determined to escape Gethsemane that he flees naked, leaving his linen cloth in the hands of the grasping mob (14:51–52).[60] Then, in a more elaborate and gut-wrenching episode, Peter denies Jesus three times, proving a disgraceful foil—a kind of "Anti-Messiah"[61]—to Jesus' truthful testimony before the high priest (14:53–65). The crowing of the cock (14:68, 72) reminds both Peter and the audience that Jesus himself promised this denial, and that Peter resisted it (14:30). With the course of divine action long determined, the foremost disciple must remain an outsider to a path that only Jesus, at this point in time (cf. 13:9–13), can walk. The Rock (Πέτρος) is now a scattered sheep.

In their anticipation of Jesus' arrest and abandonment, the scenes on the Mount of Olives and in Gethsemane reinforce the transcendent logic of Jesus' passion unlike any previous episodes. With Jesus surrounded only by enemies, however, the Gospel proceeds to reinforce its theological tension in a more balanced manner. On the one hand, then, Jesus' appearances before the Jewish council (14:53–65) and Pontius Pilate (15:1–15) illustrate Mark's invasive logic, depicting him as the victim of violent human resistance to God's encroaching reign. In the case of the former, members of the council seek a pretext for putting Jesus to death (14:55), cannot present viable and consistent evidence against him (14:56–59), yet nonetheless find grounds for condemnation in Jesus' own testimony. This comes when the high priest asks Jesus directly, "Are you the Christ, the Son of the Blessed One?" (14:62), to which Jesus responds with the theologically charged "I am" (14:62)[62] along with a bold promise of the Son of Man's return in judgment (14:62; cf. 13:24–27). Although the audience knows such testimony to be truthful, the blind leaders hear only "blasphemy" and so sentence Jesus to death (14:64).[63] The explicit assertion of his authority scandalizes their collective imagination (cf. 12:12), just as the exercise of that authority scandalized it in earlier chapters. Having now heard the assertion, however, they have the long-awaited pretext for execution (3:6).

Jesus' subsequent appearance before Pontius Pilate (15:1–15) also depicts him as the victim of human resistance and decision making, thus reinforcing Mark's invasive logic. Pilate's repeated (and clearly sarcastic) use of the phrase "King of the Jews" (15:2, 9, 12) shows that his imagination also precludes (quite understandably) the possibility of Jesus' claim to royalty. With no vested interest in Jewish squabbling, however, Pilate functions, despite his vastly superior political power, as a mere vehicle for the leaders' conspiracy. Pilate's final decision to execute Jesus stems from the overwhelming voice of the crowds, who demand the release of Barabbas instead of Jesus. Yet the crowds only give voice to the desires of the chief priests (15:9–15), so that Pilate ultimately functions as a pawn of the Jerusalem establishment.

When heard together, then, 14:53–65 and 15:1–15 depict Jesus' crucifixion as the unhappy result of a series of causes and effects, a series going all the way back to the beginning of the narrative: Jesus dies because Pilate wishes to satisfy the crowd; but the crowd demands Jesus' death because it has been stirred up by the leaders; the leaders have long opposed Jesus' authoritative ministry; yet Jesus' authoritative ministry manifests the encroachment of God's eschatological reign. Executed "with the nails of creative vapidity," Jesus is, in the end, overwhelmed by earthly resistance to God's invasive action in the world.

Yet Mark's depiction of the crucifixion itself returns hearers to the Gospel's transcendent logic through repeated references to Scripture and to Psalm 22 in particular.[64] The dividing of Jesus' clothes and casting of lots by soldiers (Mark 15:19–20) echoes Ps. 22:18. The derisive shaking of heads by onlookers (Mark 15:29) echoes Ps. 22:7. Finally, and most significantly, Jesus' final cry asserts God's transcendent will in a more direct echo of Ps. 22:1: "My God, my God, why have you forsaken me?" (Mark 15:34). As a result of these allusions the audience once again finds evidence of a divine script, though now it experiences the actual performance of the script and not just its anticipation. In the words of C. Clifton Black, Mark's scriptural allusions "suggest without directly demonstrating that, in precisely this manner of Jesus' dying, God's will is being fulfilled."[65] Events unfold this way because this is the way God has promised, so that Jesus' executioners are, with respect to God's will, "both opponents and . . . helpers."[66]

CONCLUSION

While the first half of the Gospel includes ominous references to Jesus' violent fate (1:11, 14; 2:20; 3:6; 6:14–29), the midway point clarifies that fate as "necessary" (8:31). Due to the ambiguity of this necessity, however, the audience must wrestle with possible explanations as it moves along the second half of its narrative journey. As with the dilemma of the disciples' misunderstanding in earlier chapters, hearers come to encounter two divergent possibilities for Jesus' necessary death, possibilities that again correspond to God's divergent modes of action. By the time Jesus dies, then, hearers have discerned both an invasive logic and a transcendent logic to his suffering. The passion reflects both earthly resistance to God and the foreordained script of God.

Here too one also faces the question of whether Mark's depiction of God's transcendent action suppresses, or even trumps, his depiction of God's invasive action. In other words, does the emergence of a divine script resolve whatever tension the audience might initially experience? With respect to Jesus' passion the question carries added force because God's transcendent action, in this case, marks the fulfillment of ancient scriptural promises, promises preceding the actual time of the narrative. One might reason, therefore, that even God's invasive action, along with the violent opposition it elicits, operates in accordance with God's foreordained script, so that characters function more like chess pieces than actual people. To further support this claim, one might point to a number of smaller details related to Jesus' death for which Mark provides scriptural explanation (15:19–20, 29, 34, 49–50; cf. 14:27).

This, of course, is precisely the interpretation demanded by Mark's transcendent logic. I contend, however, that the emergence of a divine script does not resolve the larger tension of Jesus' passion but is precisely what creates it. Clearly this would not be the case had Mark chosen to assert his transcendent logic at the beginning of the Gospel. For in that case hearers would naturally understand the ensuing opposition to Jesus simply as confirmation of the divine script. As it stands, however, the Gospel begins by asserting an invasive logic and follows that logic, with few exceptions, until rather late in the narrative. For although Mark raises the possibility of a transcendent logic at 8:31 and makes a direct allusion to it at 9:12, he does not drive it home until Jesus himself begins preparations for his death (14:21, 27). The emergence of this transcendent logic therefore complicates, rather than clarifies, the cause of Jesus' death, producing an outright tension at the Gospel's violent climax (14:53–15:39).

Thus the Markan passion account yields no single explanation, for God operates on two planes simultaneously. The tension of the narrative does better justice to its divine subject than any single viewpoint might, in that it preserves a middle course between two potentially dangerous (because too one-sided) interpretations of the cross. So, on the one hand, Mark's transcendent logic precludes the possibility of understanding the cross as an earthly impediment, however temporary, to God's encroaching reign—for God stands, mysteriously, behind the crucifixion itself.[67] On the other hand, Mark's invasive logic precludes the possibility of understanding the cross as an excessively violent, foreordained event, stemming from a seemingly capricious God—for the cross is also the result of the world's hostile reaction to God's presence-come-near. Taking both trajectories into consideration, one finds that Jesus' crucifixion paradoxically implies both God's vulnerability and God's sovereignty. The tension prevents us from drawing exclusively from one trajectory at the exclusion of the other.

The same is true for the way Mark implicates the disciples, who in many respects illustrate this climactic tension most acutely. The audience cannot *unreservedly* blame them for resisting Jesus' passion predictions, or for abandoning Jesus at his arrest, any more than it can *unreservedly* blame them for misunderstanding his earlier miracles.[68] A thoroughly condemnatory reading of the disciples' behavior altogether neglects Mark's transcendent logic. For while the audience empathizes with Jesus' struggle to teach them, and while it agonizes over his isolation upon their abandonment—it cannot simply write them off as utter failures or cowards. The disciples do not merely fail in their abandonment; they fail *and* fulfill divine promises. Conversely, to regard them merely as God's chess pieces undercuts Jesus' repeated teachings on discipleship—the extending of God's reign on the model of the crucified Messiah. It is to dismiss the importance of Mark's invasive logic and the disciples' sad complicity within it.

In the end, then, Mark's account of a crucified Messiah speaks not only to the limits of the human imagination within the narrative. It also, if not primarily, challenges the imaginations of the Gospel's hearers. Unlike the situation within the narrative, however, the challenge to Mark's audience presumably does not concern the authority of crucified Messiah—that is, whether Jesus could be Messiah while still undergoing suffering and death.[69] Rather, the challenge centers on the reasons for that suffering and death. In response to this question Mark gives no easy explanation but rather two irresolvable explanations. Jesus "must" die because, in the quest for self-preservation (leaders) and self-aggrandizement (disciples), "people have no alternative."[70] And Jesus must die, quite simply, because God wills it. It is precisely this "both-and" that challenges the collective imagination of the audience, drawing it more deeply into the divine mystery of the passion.[71]

5

God at/beyond the Ending
(Mark 15:40–16:8)

And going out, they fled from the tomb, for fear and amazement
seized them. And they said nothing to anyone, for they were afraid.
—*Mark 16:8*

[T]he appropriate response to the fact of the Church is gratitude.
—*Rowan Williams[1]*

Jesus' death does not end Mark's story. For at the conclusion of the Sabbath a
group of three women, intending to anoint Jesus' corpse (16:1), find that the
"very large" stone (16:4) sealing the tomb has been rolled back; and instead of
Jesus' corpse they find "a young man dressed in a white robe" (16:5). Although
the women are immediately alarmed (16:5), the angelic messenger[2] responds
with what is intended as an assuring message: "Do not be alarmed. You seek Jesus
of Nazareth, who was crucified. He has been raised; he is not here. Behold the
place where they laid him. But go, tell his disciples and Peter that he is going
ahead of you to Galilee. There you will see him, just as he told you!" (Mark
16:6–7). Thus the resurrection sets the stage for the expected completion of the
story, namely, reunion and reconciliation in Galilee, the very location where disciples were first called (1:17; 14:28) and where Jesus himself said they would meet
(14:28). Hearers may also anticipate in Galilee the final commissioning of the
disciples to preach the gospel to all nations (13:9–10) and, therefore, the full realization of Jesus' initial promise to make them fishers of people. Instead of this
anticipated ending, however, Mark gives one final and shocking account of disobedience: "And going out, they fled from the tomb, for terror and amazement
had seized them. And they said nothing to anyone, for they were afraid" (16:8).[3]

One very well may wonder whether a Gospel ending simply with a dead messiah would have been more appropriate than this. In that case Mark's hearers would have naturally concluded, based on Jesus' previous promises, that God not only raised Jesus from the dead (8:31; 9:31; 10:34) but that this resurrection gave birth to the restoration of Jesus' estranged followers (14:28) and their subsequent mission of proclamation to the nations (13:9–10). After all, a believing audience would presumably already know that the crucifixion was not the end of the larger story, that God's final word was one of life and not death, and that this life-giving message formed the backbone of its very existence as a church community. Stated simply, Mark's audience could connect the dots, viewing its own existence as indisputable proof that Mark's story continues, beyond the Gospel's termination, toward a satisfying ending.

To be sure, Mark's Gospel does end with an account of God's life-giving word: "He has been raised" (16:6). Yet the consequences of this proclamation do not produce the ending hearers expect—the ending Mark's own narrative anticipates (but omits) and his Synoptic redactors later provide.[4] This is not a traditional denouement that ties up loose ends and provides satisfactory closure. Instead, as I argue in the present chapter, Mark's abrupt conclusion creates a final and lingering theological tension, a tension that in many respects defines the Markan view of discipleship, namely, the tension between human responsibility and divine mercy. On the one hand, then, the Gospel's ending places the task of discipleship in the hands of Mark's audience, which must pick up where the characters failed. On the other hand, however, it points the audience toward the impossibility of completing such a task without the continuous empowerment of God, who overcomes human limitations and weaknesses. While one side of the tension places a charge before the audience, the other simply places it at God's mercy.

Before outlining this tension I treat some of the less convincing (though still widely circulated) interpretations of Mark's ending. This treatment is relatively brief, however, serving mainly to illuminate the "openness" of Mark's ending and to isolate the two interpretations that, in my view, prove most consistent with the Gospel's view of God and discipleship. Since both of these interpretations originate with other scholars, my primary task is simply to explain them, to argue for their interdependence, and finally to connect them to the Gospel's underlying theological tension.

PREVIOUS APPROACHES TO MARK'S ENDING

The Ending as Qualified Silence

It is not difficult to find scholars who qualify the silence described in the Gospel's final verse.[5] David Catchpole argues, for instance, that when Mark says the women said nothing "to anyone (οὐδενὶ)," what is meant is that they said nothing to anyone except the disciples.[6] Thus Catchpole envisions the women completing their mission in strict accordance with their instructions, since the young man directs them specifically to the "disciples and Peter" (16:7). In a similar vein, C. E. B. Cranfield argues that the women were only temporarily silent and that, at some indiscernible point in time, they spoke the message with which they were entrusted.[7] While Catchpole qualifies the indirect object of the sentence ("nothing"), Cranfield qualifies the direct object ("anyone," which is actually the same pronoun, οὐδείς).

Such qualifications run against the logic of Mark's rather simple grammar by misconstruing Mark's double use of the pronoun οὐδείς. The major English versions render the second οὐδείς "anyone,"[8] apparently to avoid a double negative in English.[9] Yet this translation more closely resembles the Greek pronoun τὶς, whereas οὐδείς carries the more absolute sense of *no one*. The same may be said for the use of οὐδείς as the direct object, which the NRSV appropriately translates "nothing." The repetition of the word drives home Mark's point forcefully: the women spoke nothing, and it was to no one that they spoke. It is with this absolute silence that Mark ends his Gospel.

Even accepting the logic of the grammar, it is possible (and still rather common) to qualify the silence of 16:8 based on extratextual evidence, namely, the sheer existence of the Gospel in the present day. This proves for some that someone had to have said something, for we presumably would not even have the Gospel if it had not been passed down to us through the centuries; and it could not have been passed down through the centuries had the women kept an absolute silence.[10]

This argument carries a dubious hermeneutic presupposition, however, namely, that the physical existence of the text proves a particular interpretation of its words. The argument assumes that the historical question of textual transmission determines the actual interpretation of the narrative such a text conveys. If that were the case, however, one would be forced to make the same argument even if, for example, the young man at the tomb struck the women dead ("But we have the text today, so he could not have killed them completely"). If the historical phenomenon of transmission dictates interpretation, then we have essentially robbed Mark of the freedom to write creatively and in a way that stretches the limits of historical plausibility (one might as well say, "Mark does not really depict Jesus walking on water"). As it stands, however, the narrative brackets the question of transmission, forcing the hearer/reader to adhere to its own logic, even when that logic defies the simplest (or even the most historically plausible) scenario of transmission. It seems the most one can really say, then, is that the Gospel has been handed down through the centuries *in spite of* Mark's final statement.

The Ending as Anti-Disciple Polemic

Following an altogether different line of interpretation, some have argued that Mark's ending contributes to a larger polemical agenda that Mark constructs against unidentified, though implied, opponents. The best-known of these theories, proposed by Theodore Weeden, asserts that Mark's opponents espoused a "divine man" (*theios anēr*) Christology characterized by an emphasis on "signs and wonders" (13:22).[11] Mark answers this heresy, according to Weeden, by downplaying the relevance of Jesus' miracles in regard to his true mission and by asserting Jesus' status as suffering, not glorified, Messiah. More to the point, Mark combats the divine man heresy through an altogether negative characterization of the disciples, who function in the story as its representatives. When the women flee fearfully from the tomb, then, Mark strikes his last fateful blow against his unnamed opponents. It is "the evangelist's final thrust in his vendetta against the disciples and his commitment to discredit them completely."[12]

Although Weeden's reconstruction of Mark's hypothetical opponents has yielded interesting interpretive insights, it remains to this day strictly hypothetical, based primarily on a mirror reading that Mark's Gospel never explicitly suggests. More importantly, as with any attempt to read Mark as a wholesale attack on implied opponents, Weeden cannot take into account the many exceptions to the rule he has written. For instance, although Mark certainly emphasizes Jesus as the suffering Messiah, he includes enough allusions to his future glory to render Weeden's thesis problematic (9:2–8; 13:26–27; 14:61–62).[13] Moreover, Mark's characterization of the disciples not only includes a number of positive moments within the narrative (3:13–18; 6:7–13, 30; 13:9–13) but also depicts God's own vested interest (thus generating the audience's vested interest) in their future as "fishers of people" (1:17). In the final analysis, then, a thoroughly polemic explanation of 16:8 does not align consistently enough with the story from which it purportedly stems.[14] Mark's depicts the disciples negatively, but not *this* negatively.

The Ending as Reverential Fear

Others have found a positive subtext in that the fleeing women display fear. Such fear, it is argued, suggests a kind of awed reverence before God, of which the natural and appropriate consequence is humble silence. Cranfield approaches this interpretation when he likens Mark's ending to the words of poet Isaac Watts: "God is in heaven, and men below; / Be short our tunes, our words be few; / A sacred reverence checks our songs, / And praise sits silent on our tongues."[15] The argument seems to originate, however, in the work of R. H. Lightfoot, who drew a parallel between Mark's final statement (ἐφοβοῦντο γάρ) and the "trembling and amazement" (τρόμος καὶ ἔκστασις) with which the women are seized at the beginning of 16:8.[16] Lightfoot even went so far as to posit "fear and amazement as the first and inevitable and, up to a point, right result of revelation."[17]

This line of interpretation offers promising channels of investigation, particularly with respect to the motif of amazement and awe in the larger narrative. Yet as Andrew Lincoln has shown, close attention to Mark's precise language produces rather different conclusions.[18] Analyzing 16:8 in light of the eleven other occurrences of fear (φοβέομαι, ἔκφοβος) in the Gospel, Lincoln writes: "There is no dispute that terms such as amazement, awe, trembling, and fear are frequently used [in Mark] to describe the response to an epiphany or to divine revelation of some sort. The question is whether 'fear' in Mark depicts a positive or a negative response. It turns out that in fact in Mark it usually does not depict a proper response of faith."[19]

Lincoln's argument draws from basic concordance work, the simplicity of which makes his conclusion all the more convincing. At 4:40–41, Jesus connects the disciples' fear of the storm with their lack of faith, a connection buttressed by Mark's subsequent commentary: "They feared a great fear." At 5:15 those who see the Gerasene demoniac sitting "clothed and in his right mind" are so "afraid" that "they began to beg him [Jesus] to leave their region" (5:17). At 5:36, immediately before healing Jairus's daughter, Jesus again contrasts fear with faith: "Do not fear but rather believe." At 6:50, after the disciples show terror at Jesus walking on water, Jesus attempts to correct their response: "Take courage! It is I! Do not be afraid!" This connection between fear and misunderstanding continues at 9:6, when Mark explains Peter's request to stay on the mount of the transfiguration: "He did not know what to say, for they were frightened." Mark 9:32 gives a nearly identical explanation of the disciples' reaction to Jesus' second passion: "But they did not understand what he was saying, and they were afraid to ask him." Then, immediately before Jesus' third and final prediction, Mark again says that "those who followed were afraid" (10:32). Though without any explicit connection to misunderstanding, the larger context of 8:27–10:41, with its strong emphasis on the disciples' misunderstanding, brings negative connotations to this verse as well. Finally, Mark connects fear with Jesus' enemies, first as a motive for killing him (11:18) and then as a motive for not killing him (because of the crowds, 11:32; 12:12).

The two remaining instances of fear prove more ambiguous. Herod's fear of John the Baptist (6:20) motivates his protection of him; yet one must also consider that Herod had John murdered. The "fear and trembling" of the hemorrhaging woman (5:33) may suggest the motivation for her coming forward to Jesus; yet one could just as easily construe the Greek participles (φοβηθεῖσα καὶ τρέμουσα) in an adversative sense, so that she comes forward despite her fear: "And the woman, *though* fearful and trembling . . . came and told him the truth." I prefer this translation because it reinforces the connection between speech and faith implied in Jesus' response—"Daughter, your faith has made you well" (5:34)—while also supporting the more explicit contrast between faith and fear that Jesus mentions to Jairus only two verses later (5:36).

However one treats these two ambiguous verses, Lincoln's work deals a considerable blow to the line of interpretation originating with Lightfoot. For if Mark's earlier use of fear language is any indication, then his final statement hardly suggests an awed reverence before God, much less a humble silence. It is rather more akin to faithlessness and misunderstanding—the very response hearers have come to expect from Jesus' followers.

The Ending as Hopeful: The Female Remnant

But are all followers of Jesus the same? In particular, does the presence of women at the tomb—as opposed to men—serve as a sign of hope, or at least a subtle hint, that things will not end as they appear to have ended?[20] Along these lines it is worth noting that these are the same women mentioned at 15:40, the only followers of Jesus to show their faces at his crucifixion. Moreover, Mark mentions in that scene that they "served" Jesus (διηκόνουν αὐτῷ, 15:41) during his ministry, a very positive retrospection that echoes Jesus' last teaching on true discipleship: "For the Son of Man came not to be served but to serve" (γὰρ ὁ υἱὸς τοῦ ἀνθρώπου οὐκ ἦλθεν διακονηθῆναι ἀλλὰ διακονῆσαι, 15:41). They seem not only to have understood but also to have followed the very teaching that Jesus' male disciples consistently resisted.[21]

If we set this group alongside other female characters in the Gospel, a very encouraging possibility emerges. For with the single exception of Herodias, wife of Herod (6:17–29), Mark casts women in a consistently positive light. Simon's mother-in-law, who is among the first people Jesus heals (1:30–31), responds to her healing by "serving" (διακονέω; cf. 10:45; 15:41). The hemorrhaging woman shows great faith and is also healed (5:25–34). The Syrophoenician woman challenges Jesus to heal her daughter (7:25–30) and actually wins the debate. The poor widow gives her whole life despite her poverty (12:41–44). Finally, an unnamed woman anoints Jesus' body for burial (14:3–9), giving rise to unparalleled praise from Jesus: "Wherever the good news is proclaimed in the whole world, what she has done will be told in remembrance of her" (14:9). By the time Mark's audience reaches the crucifixion, then, it should not be surprised to hear of women modeling discipleship.

Yet in assessing the significance of this remnant, one must still consider its actions. At the crucifixion, for instance, the women observe Jesus only "from a distance" (ἀπὸ μακρόθεν, 15:40), the same way Peter followed Jesus "from a distance" into the courtyard of the high priest only to deny him three times (14:66–72). Observing from a distance also places the women in stark contrast to those who mock Jesus up close (15:25–32), reminding hearers of Jesus' first teaching on true discipleship: "If anyone wants to follow behind me, let them deny themselves and *take up their cross* and follow me" (8:34). When heard against the background of this teaching, the women do not seem obedient at all. An attentive audience will note Mark's crucial qualification: "They followed him *when he was in Galilee*" (ὅτε ἦν ἐν τῇ Γαλιλαίᾳ, 15:41). Even if this female remnant exhibits greater endurance and a more praiseworthy history than the male disciples, they hardly represent "the glow of dawn after a dark night."[22] Rather they accentuate Jesus' utter isolation.

This is quite apart from the women's actions at the empty tomb. For it is here that their behavior conclusively defies whatever positive expectations the Gospel has created for women. They "flee" the empty tomb just as the male disciples flee the Garden of Gethsemane (ἔφυγον, 14:50, 52); and in fleeing they speak "nothing to anyone," in blatant disregard for the messenger's instructions. In the end, then, Mark's female remnant signifies not a cloaked assertion of hope to which the audience holds optimistically, but rather an ironic challenge to the very expectations the audience has come to place in women. Along these lines Elizabeth Struthers Malbon insightfully notes how 16:8 incorporates women followers into a truly Markan view of discipleship since, in the end, they prove to be "fallible followers" just like the apostles themselves.[23] As women they show the audience how discipleship is not an exclusively male calling. As *fallible* women, however, they represent the equally Markan idea that all followers of Jesus—whether male or female—remain susceptible to misunderstanding and failure. Just as disciple membership knows no boundaries, so too does disciple failure.

HONORING THE LOGIC OF MARK'S ENDING

The Openness of the Ending

Although they each raise important questions, the above interpretations attempt to salvage 16:8 from its own unsatisfying logic: outright disobedience in the form of flight and silence. In this way they reflect a characteristic common to the history of interpretation of this verse, namely, an anxiety over openness. Frank Kermode goes so far as calling this anxiety a pervasive tendency with respect to all literature, a tendency manifesting itself in forced attempts at closure. When interpreting a text, we are inclined to "accommodate the discrepancies and dissonances into some larger scheme," or to "argue away inconvenient portions," all out of the unstated conviction that everything must "hang together."[24] Stated simply, when a text does not achieve closure we create it for ourselves. When we cannot create it, we often disregard the stories themselves as "bad literature" (Mark's own reception history being a prime example[25]).

This is not a categorical rejection of closure as such. My point is only that the ending of this particular Gospel denies us the closure we naturally seek, and that a truly Markan experience of that ending should honor its openness. That Matthew and Luke resisted this openness is obvious from their respective redactions of Mark's ending.[26] That Mark's own transmitters resisted it is obvious from the various scribal additions that soon followed the Gospel's circulation.[27] That Mark's modern interpreters have resisted it is obvious from the exegetical gymnastics consistently performed in an attempt to soften the offense of his final sentence.[28] Within the history of interpretation, then, one finds a consistent dissatisfaction that essentially proves Kermode's claim, a refusal to believe that the women really "said nothing to anyone."

So, in an effort to resist this tendency, I second Richard Swanson's contention that "Mark's story will always be misread whenever [this] offense becomes domesticated."[29] At the same time, however, one must note that the openness of Mark's ending is not entirely offensive, since the disappointment of 16:8 is in many respects balanced by the good news of 16:6–7. Indeed, the resurrection of Jesus (16:6) and his waiting in Galilee (16:7) fulfill perhaps the most important promises of the narrative: Life will overcome death (8:31; 9:31; 10:34) and will enable the redemption of failed followers (14:28).[30] Having experienced the violent humiliation of Golgotha, hearers cannot help but rejoice over the vindication of Jesus and his merciful devotion to the disciples.

The reliability of Jesus as a prophet is well established, at least for Mark's audience, even before the announcement at 16:6–7. Smaller predictions have already been fulfilled, such as Jesus' instructions for preparation (11:2–7; 14:12–16) and his cursing of the fig tree (11:12–14, 20–21). Most significantly, Jesus' passion has unfolded precisely as he foretold, particularly with respect to his third and most detailed prediction (10:33–34). In this way the fulfillment of 16:6–7 simply confirms a reliability that hearers have long acknowledged. When Jesus says something will happen, hearers expect it to happen, if not over the course of the narrative then at some point beyond it.

Those promises lingering beyond the end of the narrative are of no small consequence: the reunion between Jesus and the disciples (14:28), the subsequent testimony and persecution of the disciples (13:9–10), and the final endtime events (13:1–37) that culminate with the coming of the Son of Man (13:26–27; 14:62) and the consummation of God's reign (4:20–32; 9:1). Those same promises also contain a plethora of details. Thus, with respect to the disciples, they will be handed over to councils, beaten in synagogues, and made to stand before earthly rulers (13:9–10). With respect to the end times, they will involve wars and rumors of wars (13:7–8), widespread suffering (13:14–20), false messiahs (13:5–6, 21–22), betrayal (13:12), and various cosmic phenomena (13:8, 24–25). Such details lend an element of believability, especially for an audience already prone to trust Jesus, and especially after that same audience experiences the fulfillment of other detailed promises.

In this way Mark creates "a momentum that drives [hearers] beyond the ending into the period beyond the story."[31] Consequently, the audience's experience of the Gospel's ending is not equivalent to its experience of its final verse. If the audience has experienced the entire Gospel, in other words, then it encounters Mark's ending while still holding on to whatever "loose ends" remain beyond that ending. Since these "loose ends" consist of unfulfilled promises made by an altogether reliable prophet, the audience can expect Mark's larger story to end differently than his actual Gospel. There is even a sense in which the audience *knows* the ending of the story. As Jesus himself says, "they *will* hand you over (παραδώσουσιν ὑμᾶς) to councils, and you *will* be beaten (δαρήσεσθε) in synagogues" (13:9), and "they *will* see (ὄψονται) the Son of Man coming in clouds with great glory and power" (13:26). Coming in the wake of such trustworthy promises, 16:6–7 does not simply proclaim good news for the present; it also anticipates events with which the audience is already familiar.[32]

This does not mean, however, that the good news of 16:6–7 resolves the dilemma created by 16:8, as if the mere fact of the resurrection, or the mere fact of Jesus' going to Galilee, somehow softened the reality of the women's absolute silence.[33] Such a conclusion would seriously underestimate the dilemma itself, because the logic of 16:8 flies in the face of those promises.[34] Resurrection is supposed to lead to proclamation (9:9), proclamation is supposed to lead to reunion and restoration, and restoration will presumably lead to the realization of true discipleship. Yet these expected transitions never occur because there is no proclamation in the first place. Precisely when "the story seems salvageable,"[35] 16:8 throws a "monkey wrench into the machinery."[36]

It would be more appropriate to say that the salvaging of the story will *not* take place—at least not at the hands of the women, who are the only characters (aside from the angelic messenger) aware of Jesus' resurrection![37] Arriving at the end of its narrative journey, then, the audience finds that the breaking of silence has been entrusted to those who do not speak. In the words of Lincoln, "they are to tell of a promise that failure is not the end, but then *they* fail to tell and that *is* the end—of the narrative!"[38] In this way the Gospel concludes on a note of profound tension, and with an unforgettable testament to the disciples' fallibility: the opportunity for redemption has been offered, only to be squandered.

An Openness That Commissions the Audience

The future has been refused by characters but not by the Gospel's hearers. This distinction is crucial, since it raises the possibility that 16:8, while throwing a "monkey wrench" into the machinery of the narrative, need not have an identical effect outside the narrative. Indeed, there is a sense in which the "dilemma" created by Mark's last sentence functions positively with respect to one of the Gospel's primary goals: the fostering of discipleship on the model of Christ. The disobedient silence of Mark's female remnant serves as an implied commission to the audience to step in and finish the story itself.

First articulated by Mary Ann Tolbert,[39] this interpretation accounts for the tension of Mark's ending, and in a manner consistent with the larger narrative. In terms of tension, it honors both the jarring logic of 16:8 and the reliability of Jesus' lingering promises. The women's silence is not temporary, their fear is not praiseworthy, and their gender is not ultimately a cause of hope. They really do flee in disobedient and absolute silence, taking the news of Jesus' resurrection with them. At the same time, however, their behavior need not prevent the proclamation of the gospel since Jesus' followers are not confined to the world of the narrative. The audience, therefore, must break the silence of 16:8 and anticipate the public testimony promised at 13:9–13.

This is not just a clever hermeneutic tactic but an interpretation grounded in the logic of the Gospel. For even in the face of the disciples' resistance, Jesus teaches continuously on the nature of true discipleship. Moreover, it is precisely in these teachings that Jesus uses his most universal tone, employing his characteristic relative pronouns to pull the audience into the story: "*Whoever* does the will of God is my brother and sister and mother" (3:35). "If *anyone* wishes to follow me let them deny themselves, take up their cross, and follow me. For *whoever* wishes to save his life will lose it, and *whoever* wishes to lose his life because of me and the gospel will save it" (8:34–35). "*Whoever* wishes to be first must be last of all and servant of all" (9:35). "*Whoever* receives one such child in my name receives me, and *whoever* receives me receives not me but the one who sent me" (9:37). "*Whoever* wishes to be great among you must be your servant, and *whoever* wishes to be first among you must be servant of all" (10:43–44).

In the words of Tolbert, then, there is a sense in which "Mark has created in the role of the authorial audience the perfect disciple."[40] Through their experience of the Gospel, hearers learn what it means (and what it takes) to follow Jesus and, therefore, how to avoid the failings of characters in the narrative—not just the silence of the female remnant but also, and more fundamentally, the worldly priorities of Peter and the rest of the disciples. Stated simply, the Gospel equips hearers to finish the discipleship story in a manner worthy of Jesus' vision. They are, like the Galilean fishermen, called to extend God's transformative reign into the world.

Jesus, however, remains the primary model for following this call, if only because the Gospel treats his ministry much more extensively than it does the disciples. Particularly in the first half of the Gospel (1:21–8:26), the audience encounters the kinds of actions that Jesus will later define as "serving" (9:35; 10:43–45). He heals, feeds, enters into fellowship, casts out demons, and, through all these actions, alleviates the suffering of others with unwavering compassion. In short, he brings God's transformative reign. Thus the call of discipleship is not simply a matter of preaching but also a matter of bringing wholeness to a broken world. Indeed, the model of Jesus suggests that the bringing of wholeness *is* the proclamation of God's encroaching reign.[41]

An Openness That Points to God's Mercy

Tolbert's interpretation, or some form of it, has gradually come to dominate the scholarly literature on Mark's ending.[42] In my view, however, an interpretation that leans exclusively on human effort does not reflect a truly Markan understanding of discipleship. For the Gospel has stressed not only the necessity and consequences of following the crucified Messiah but also the utter fallibility of those called to follow. Indeed, more than the other evangelists Mark emphasizes the ugly side of discipleship, the tendency of followers to misunderstand, resist, fear, distrust, and even abandon Jesus. This is particularly the case when it comes to the issue of Jesus' "necessary" passion—the very issue that defines the task of discipleship. From the moment this necessity surfaces in the narrative, the disciples begin to exhibit a worldview diametrically opposed to the self-giving service required of them (8:32–33; 9:33–34; 10:13–16, 35–37). In fact, they no longer fulfill their vocation at all (cf. 6:7–13, 30–44; 8:1–10; 9:14–29).

As noted in chapter four, although the scripting of the disciples' final abandonment prevents the audience's wholesale denunciation of them, it also does not provide a wholesale excuse for them. It does not lessen the sense of fallibility most evident on the way to Caesarea Philippi (8:27–9:1) and in subsequent episodes. For it is there that the audience sees most clearly how Jesus' followers think "the things of humans" rather than "the things of God." Even if the vindication of Jesus' suffering, through his resurrection, should convert the disciples to God's perspective (as suggested by 9:9; 13:9–13), the

Gospel gives no indication whatsoever that such conversion would overcome, entirely and conclusively, the lure of the human perspective. Along these lines, the Gospel also does not suggest that the audience stands a better chance of fulfilling its discipleship vocation than the characters. Hearers may learn from the disciples' mistakes, but this does not necessarily protect them from the same temptations.[43]

Viewed from this perspective one must question whether Mark has simply "handed over" his story to the audience, as if Jesus' lingering promises were somehow attainable by strictly human means. An audience attuned to God's action in the narrative will note that such action bears directly upon the discipleship vocation—nor is this merely a matter of divine initiative in calling the disciples (1:16–20) and bestowing them with authority (3:13–15). More fundamentally, Mark indicates that the very task of discipleship—the realization of Jesus' teachings—requires divine help. Jesus, after all, does not command Simon (Peter) and Andrew to become fishers of people but rather promises them, "I *will make you* (ποιήσω ὑμᾶς) become fishers of people" (1:17). The window into discipleship given at 13:9–13 follows the same logic, promising rather than commanding the disciples' future testimony and suffering, including even a reference to divine empowerment via the Holy Spirit (13:11).

It is not enough, therefore, to say simply that Mark's ending commissions the audience to break the women's silence. Precisely because the task of discipleship requires divine help, such commissioning also, and necessarily, places the audience at the mercy of God. Much like the disciples facing a hungry crowd in the desert, hearers find themselves called to a task they cannot do through their own powers: "*You* feed them" (6:37). In one sense, then, it is a task "riddled through and through with anxiety,"[44] an anxiety multiplied by promises of violent worldly resistance (13:9, 12–13; cf. 6:14–29). Yet for the audience that recognizes, based on its experience of the Gospel, the role of God in the larger story, it is also a task that promises divine assistance: "Whatever things for which you pray and ask, trust that you have received them, and it will be yours" (11:24). "Do not worry beforehand about what you will say; but say whatever is given to you in that hour" (13:11).

In this way Mark's ending commissions the audience not only to act but to remember—to remember its own shortcomings and, more fundamentally, the power of God to overcome them. Stated simply, the audience must remember that its collective action on Christ's behalf is not exclusively its own. For the task of discipleship is no normal task but rather an extension of God's encroaching reign into the world, and precisely for that reason it points the listening community to the merciful God who transcends it. It is "as if someone would scatter seed on the ground, and would sleep and rise night and day, and the seed would sprout and grow—he does not know how" (4:26–27).

CONCLUSION

If there was ever an ending that was not an ending, this is it. More significantly, it is not an ending in a very surprising way. For the audience has been prepared for Jesus' resurrection just as much as it has been prepared for his passion (8:31; 9:9, 31; 10:33–34), and it has been encouraged to associate that resurrection with the beginning of the disciples' proclamation (9:9; 13:9–13). The rather detailed account of Jesus' burial by Joseph of Arimathea (15:42–47), coupled with the appearance of women at the tomb (16:1), builds on this momentum by putting all the pieces in place: it is time for the risen Jesus to appear, and it is time for the disciples to begin preaching (14:28). To the extent that Mark's audience already knows some oral tradition(s) concerning Jesus' resurrection (e.g., 1 Cor. 15:1–8), the sense of anticipation will be heightened even more.

The good news, of course, is that Jesus is indeed raised. But the surprising news, at least for the audience, is that the expected transition from resurrection to proclamation does not happen. More to the point, the logic of Mark's final statement suggests that such a transition has been rendered impossible—at least so far as human characters are concerned. Or, stated differently, it denies the very existence of the Markan community except on exclusively theological grounds. If the audience wants to connect its existence to the Markan Jesus, then, it must posit nothing less than a divine miracle, since it is only for God that "all things are possible" (14:36).[45] Indeed, it is precisely because all things are possible for Mark's God that one need not, and should not, assume that Mark's ending means anything other than what it says: "They said nothing to anyone" (16:8).[46] To hear such an ending is to experience the truth in Rowan Williams's claim that "the appropriate response to the fact of the Church is gratitude."[47]

All the more reason to insist that Mark's ending points the audience to God's mercy and not simply to itself. In a sense the favoring of one party, at the exclusion of the other, amounts to the kind of forced closure that Kermode laments and the Gospel's ending logically precludes.[48] It is simply to follow in the footsteps of Mark's redactors and transmitters, replacing the mystery (and potential messiness) of an untold divine-human encounter with a more intelligible and satisfying "single meaning." Both the audience and God are indispensable, then, for a truly Markan consideration of the story's continuation. This does not "explain away" that continuation, however, any more than Mark "explains" the miraculous feeding of multitudes (6:30–44; 8:1–10). It is merely to state the nature of the mystery itself, and to state it in terms consistent with the preceding Markan narrative: the God who transcends the listening community will continue to act invasively, extending his reign through, and sometimes in spite of, the actions of fallible humans.

Along these lines it is worth noting how the tension of Mark's ending reflects, albeit indirectly, the underlying theological tension of the entire Gospel, with the audience implicated now more than ever before. Since the task of discipleship is a matter of extending God's transformative reign into the world, the commission implied by the ending points the audience toward its collective participation in God's invasive action. Since that very commission points to the need for God's own mercy, however, it also points the audience toward God's transcendent action. In other words, the audience cannot collapse its view of God into its own ministry; for even though God continues to act through that ministry, God cannot be equated exhaustively with it. God remains the object of prayer and inspiration (11:24; 13:11), the transcendent source for God's own encroachment via human agents.

Conclusion

Accentuating the Mystery of Mark's Gospel

In following God through Mark I have emphasized God's role as the Gospel's main actor and the way God's divergent modes of action come to bear upon the actions of Jesus and his disciples. While I think it unnecessary to rehearse these arguments, I do want to elaborate on two broad areas of discussion, highlighting the primary contributions I hope to have made to the field of Markan studies.

MARK'S AUDIENCE AND THE MYSTERY OF GOD

If you understand him, he is not God.

—Saint Augustine[1]

Above all, I want to bring attention to the element of divine mystery in the Gospel as it is expressed in God's divergent modes of action. On the few occasions that scholars have focused on Mark's characterization of God, they have either limited the investigation to explicit God-language (overlooking more implicit means of characterization within the narrative) or gravitated toward only one mode of divine activity. The latter tendency stems largely from the unspoken assumption of univocal meaning, and in this respect my contribution is hermeneutic. At the end of the day, however, it is not enough simply to question hermeneutic presuppositions and forward interpretive possibilities. One must also argue the case through exegesis. It is my hope that I have done this persuasively, demonstrating how Mark simultaneously depicts God's invasive and transcendent action vis-à-vis Jesus.

I also hope to have shown how a focus on this primary tension brings to light, or helps to explain, still other tensions. The initial following of the disciples reflects both a human volition and an irresistible divine attraction. The disciples' misunderstanding of Jesus' miracles stems both from human obduracy and divine hardening. Jesus' passion stems both from human resistance to his ministry and God's own will as recorded in Scripture. The disciples abandon Jesus both because they wish to save themselves and because they are scripted into the divine plan. With each of these narrative developments the audience receives two logically irresolvable explanations, one attributed ultimately to God's invasive action, the other to God's transcendent action. Both sides of each tension are rather easily understood, but *as tensions* they are not. God's activity is everywhere, yet it is essentially mystery.

I use the word "mystery" because I presuppose a believing audience already inclined to trust Mark's God and Mark's Jesus—an audience that will not allow the experience of tension to undermine its belief in God's reliability and faithfulness. To highlight what is at stake in this presupposition, it is worth comparing my interpretation to the work of Philip Reubin Johnson, who reads the Gospel with similar questions.[2] In focusing on the relationship between God and Jesus, Johnson charts a gradual yet decisive transition from their "inseparability" to their "separability."[3] The climactic conclusion to this transition comes at Jesus' cry of dereliction (15:34), when the audience, according to Johnson, must ask whether God, based on his alarming silence and inaction, actually loves Jesus as previously claimed (1:11).[4] Johnson goes so far as to call this a moment of "inner conflict"[5] for God, with the result that the audience experiences the crucifixion scene with "antipathy" toward the distant Father.

Johnson is right to implicate God in the suffering and death of Jesus. But his analysis reveals how drastically different one will assess the passion when a different kind of audience is presupposed. Johnson posits the kind of "implied reader" common to structuralist-minded interpretation, the kind that exists "in" the text and that "reads" the Gospel, so to speak, with an entirely neutral stance toward the God and Scripture, not to mention out of complete ignorance of the gospel message as a whole. This kind of implied reader begins the narrative as a blank slate and learns about God and Jesus only what the actual words of the narrative tell her.

There is no need to repeat here my theoretical objections to this kind of reader (see the introduction). I suppose the audience I have assumed better resembles the scholarly consensus on Mark's "original" audience; it certainly resembles the kinds of audiences the Gospel quickly acquired, first by virtue of its transmission within the early church and then by virtue of its gradual canonization. My primary objective, however, is not to debate the issue of audience but to highlight the resulting difference in how one gauges God's complicity in Jesus' passion. For if the Gospel does presume a believing audience predisposed to trust the God of Jesus—perhaps even one loosely familiar with the story of Jesus—then the tensions of the narrative, I believe, will speak more toward God's mystery than God's "inner conflict." If that is the case, the audience will be considerably less likely to experience those tensions with antipathy toward God. The tensions may certainly generate a renewed sense of God's incomprehensibility or a heightened sense of awe, and they may certainly challenge the audience's prior understanding of God and God's relationship to Jesus. But as the tensions are basic elements of a story Mark calls "the good news" of Jesus Christ, it seems most improbable that they are intended to evoke antipathy.

Along these lines it is worth noting at least one episode within the narrative that supports this interpretation: the confrontation between Jesus and Peter on the way to Caesarea Philippi (8:31–33). For it is Peter who, in his rebuke of Jesus' necessary passion, expresses antipathy toward "the things of God." And it is Jesus who opposes, and exposes, the logic of Peter's antipathy, precisely by aligning his passion with "the things of God." Here God certainly defies expectations; but God does not, Mark suggests, contradict his self-proclaimed love for Jesus (1:11). Rather, God expresses that love in the very next scene to the disciples: "This is my Son, the *Beloved* [ὁ ἀγαπητός]. Listen to him!" (9:7). Whether to challenge or to reassure, then, the Gospel presents the audience with a profound tension: Jesus is loved by God, and Jesus' death is willed by God. Peter must learn that living with this mystery is a reality of following Jesus. Antipathy, he does learn, results in abandonment.

This is not to deny the sharp contrast, logically speaking, between the close identification of Jesus and God in the prologue, on the one hand, and the disturbing silence that follows Jesus' final cry, on the other hand (15:34). Indeed, when gauged in terms of an audience's temporal and dynamic experience, the God/Jesus subplot does include significant developments. But the idea of a strictly linear development from "inseparability" to "separability" is ruled out, in my view, by God's initial possession of Jesus, a possession implied throughout the narrative but that does not factor into Johnson's interpretation.[6] Due to this continued possession (ironically referenced in the debate of 3:20–30), whatever friction arising between Jesus and God will create tension for the audience and will therefore enhance its sense of divine mystery. Within the narrative, however, it does not replace or trump Jesus' previous alignment with God. Rather it will profoundly complicate the relationship itself, or, to be more specific, it will complicate the audience's view of that relationship.

Mark reminds hearers of this continued possession at the crucifixion itself when Jesus, "giving out a great cry, breathed out" (15:37). While the reference to "breathing out" (ἐξέπνευσεν) functions as a euphemism for Jesus' death, its literal sense echoes God's initial "putting in" of the Spirit (τὸ πνεῦμα . . . καταβαῖνον εἰς αὐτόν, 1:10), especially when one considers how previous

"great cries" (φωνὴν μεγάλην) have occurred only in cases of spiritual possession and exorcism (1:26; 5:7; cf. 15:34).[7] More to the point, this breathing out
occurs *after* the cry of dereliction (15:37), that is, after the most pronounced
indication of so-called separability in the entire narrative. This suggests that
Jesus' possession has continued even through the crucifixion itself. The Spirit
leaves only at the point of death; or perhaps the leaving of the Spirit allows for
death. Either way, it is surely no coincidence that Jesus' expiration leads immediately to the tearing of the temple curtain, indicating that the Father is hardly
distant, much less absent, from the scene, and that the death of the Son will
not halt the action of the Father.

For all of these reasons I liken Mark's Gospel to the words of Augustine: "If
you understand him, he is not God."[8] It is certainly not that the Gospel fails to
speak about God. From beginning to end it imparts what might be called knowledge of God. But what the audience comes to know about God it cannot ultimately comprehend, for this knowledge is grounded in irresolvable tension. In
hearing this theological tension, the audience experiences the divine mystery.

MARK'S AUDIENCE AND THE MYSTERY
OF DISCIPLESHIP

> But the LORD is with me like a dread warrior.
> *—Jeremiah 20:11 NRSV*

A believing audience, I have also argued, will hold a vested interest in Mark's
characterization of the disciples, not only because it considers itself a community of disciples but also because Mark depicts God's own vested interest in the
disciples (1:17; 13:9–13; 14:28). In this way one cannot wholly isolate Mark's
characterization of the disciples from his characterization of God, or, more
specifically, the actions of one party from the other. For the disciples are
caught, so to speak, between God's divergent modes of action, so that the audience discerns no single explanation, but rather divergent explanations, for why
Jesus is followed, feared, misunderstood, and abandoned. Even with respect to
the disciples, then, Mark's discourse draws hearers deeper into the mystery of
God. One might even say, on the model of Augustine, that if we understand
them they are not Mark's disciples.

This argument I hope will advance the scholarly conversation by bringing
to light an overlooked theological dimension in the disciple subplot. As Hanson notes, current discussions tend to gravitate toward one of two interpretive
camps, each of which tries to account for Mark's largely negative depiction of
the disciples.[9] Advocates of the so-called polemical reading argue that Mark

wants hearers to reject the disciples and their worldview in favor of Jesus.[10] Advocates of the so-called pastoral reading argue that Mark wants hearers to identify with the disciples in their failures and, through that identification, experience encouragement themselves.[11]

Admitting a degree of generalization, I follow Hanson's critique of both camps. While the polemical reading recognizes the severity of Mark's portrait of the disciples, it cannot account for the positive glimpses Mark gives of the disciples, or, more fundamentally, God's own vested interest in them. While the pastoral reading recognizes the disciples' positive moments and God's faithfulness to them, it cannot account for the severity of their negative moments, as Hanson notes: "the disciples do not need to be quite so obdurate."[12] Indeed, if Mark intends only to encourage his audience, then they need not be *nearly* so obdurate. In the end, then, both camps emphasize some features of the narrative at the expense of other features.

Hanson forwards a mediating position that emphasizes God's vested interest in the disciples while also honoring the severity of the disciples' failure. According to Hanson, Mark depicts the disciples so negatively precisely in order to highlight the sovereign and irresistible grace of God. The Gospel "graphically portrays the lack of a future for the world without God's intervention, but it puts no one in a position to lay exclusive claim to it. It is God's action that creates a future for the disciples, and a future for the world."[13] Thus it is not simply a matter of polemical commentary, nor simply a matter of pastoral encouragement, but also, and indeed primarily, a matter of placing God front and center as the sole source of redemption.

As with my treatment of Johnson, I mention Hanson's interpretation as a way of highlighting the distinctive features of my own. In placing God front and center Hanson provides one of the more theologically insightful readings of the disciple subplot yet to be offered. At the same time, however, he gives no real weight to God's transcendent action within the narrative and toward the disciples in particular—and here of course he is not alone. But attention to this element of the narrative brings an element of mystery to the disciple subplot, such that one cannot say only that God acts "in spite of" the disciples. For it is also the case that God hardens the disciples and, with respect to their final abandonment, writes them into the script of Jesus' passion. Such actions are both failures and not failures. The disciple subplot is a mystery because the God of the Gospel is a mystery.

In placing God front and center one also risks overshadowing the imperative of Jesus' many discipleship teachings to the point that only God, and not the audience, factors into the continuation of the story. Divine action appears simply to trump human action, instead of divine action empowering human action. But part of the beauty and mystery of Mark's Gospel lies precisely in its refusal to concede one side of this tension to the other. Without wanting to diminish Hanson's interpretation, then, I would simply want to complement it by drawing attention to the larger tension of divine mercy and human commission. For the Gospel not only anticipates human failure, and it not only promises that God will overcome that failure; it also demands human action modeled on the self-giving ministry of Jesus. After all, it is surely no coincidence that God speaks from heaven precisely when the disciples' resistance to these teachings begins to surface: "Listen to him!" (9:7). There is both impossibility and responsibility.

Yet the mystery here is not merely a matter of antithesis. It is also a matter of comfort, and this is why I have chosen to use the term "empowerment" when describing the mystery of discipleship in Mark. Consider once again the promise of 13:11: "When they bring you to trial and hand you over, do not worry beforehand about what you are to say; but say whatever is given you at that time, for it is not you who speak, but the Holy Spirit." This is more than a metaphysical rumination on the divine presence at work in the life of the believer. Nor is it simply a promise of true discipleship realized, finally, beyond the time of the narrative. Coming alongside guarantees of beatings (13:9), betrayal (13:12), and hatred (13:13), it is also an attempt to alleviate the anxiety any flesh-and-blood disciple would experience when faced with the repercussions of following Jesus, particularly given that such repercussions cause people to "fall away" (σκανδαλίζω, 4:17).

Of course, on the one hand this simply returns us to the question of whether full obedience to Jesus' teachings—denying oneself and picking up one's cross (8:34)—is even possible without God's help. Perhaps for Mark human resistance to "the things of God" stems not only from the cognitive challenge they pose but also from the prospects of actually experiencing them. If so, then it is all the more appropriate that Jesus balance his command to "endure to the end" (13:13) with the assurance of divine empowerment. At the same time, however, one must recognize the promise precisely as assurance, for assurance is, in many respects, a kind of motivation: Do not let your anxiety over this awesome responsibility prevent you from following Jesus all the way, for God is there to help you. The promise of divine mercy does not merely anticipate God's overcoming of people's self-preserving tendencies; it also acknowledges the responsibility inherent in enduring. Stated differently, that disciples are called to an impossible task does not diminish that they are called and, consequently, must respond. That is the mystery of discipleship that spills into the life of the audience.

One may liken this mystery to the words of Jeremiah, who testifies to elements of responsibility, anxiety, and divine empowerment in his own ministry:

O LORD, you have enticed me, and I was enticed; you have overpowered me, and you have prevailed. I have become a laughingstock all day long; everyone mocks me. For whenever I speak, I must cry out, I must shout, "Violence and destruction!" For the word of the LORD has become for me a reproach and derision all day long. If I say, "I will not mention him, or speak any more in his name," then within me there is something like a burning fire shut up in my bones; I am weary with holding it in, and I cannot. For I hear many whispering: "Terror is all around! Denounce him! Let us denounce him!" All my close friends are watching for me to stumble. "Perhaps he can be enticed, and we can prevail against him, and take our revenge on him." But the LORD is with me like a dread warrior; therefore my persecutors will stumble, and they will not prevail. They will be greatly shamed, for they will not succeed. Their eternal dishonor will never be forgotten. O LORD of hosts, you test the righteous, you see the heart and the mind; let me see your retribution upon them, for to you I have committed my cause (Jer. 20:7–12 NRSV).

Much like Mark, Jeremiah knows the violent and inevitable backlash of proclaiming God's word, just as he knows the dreadful anxiety such backlash can create. Within this context of resistance and anxiety Jeremiah describes his vocation with a tension strikingly similar to Mark's Gospel. On the one hand, he hears the call to proclaim God's word, and he cowers in the face of the opposition his mission inevitably elicits. More to the point, it is precisely his anxiety that accentuates the need for obedience. On the other hand, however, he testifies to God's empowering presence that, despite his own self-protective impulse, renders him incapable of silence. It is presumably this experience of divine fidelity that, in turn, inspires Jeremiah's further confidence in, and obedience to, God: "But the LORD is with me like a dread warrior; therefore my persecutors will stumble, and they will not prevail . . . for to you I have committed my cause" (Jer. 20:11–12 NRSV).

This is not an argument for Mark's dependence on Jeremiah but simply a theological reflection aimed at accentuating the tension of responsibility and impossibility inherent in the Markan view of discipleship. At the very least, one can confidently say that Mark has not arrived at an altogether new understanding of discipleship's inherent dangers, the anxiety those dangers create, and, most importantly, the role of God in overcoming such obstacles. It is in reading Mark alongside Jeremiah that one begins to sense a possible purpose, or at least a fortunate consequence, of Mark's theological view of discipleship: to foster obedience to God by accentuating God's own faithfulness. "Follow behind me," Jesus commands, "and *I will make* you to become fishers of people" (1:17).

Given that God's action within the narrative often sets the disciples at odds with their commission (if only for the purpose of realizing Jesus' passion), such an assertion of divine fidelity is crucial, particularly for the audience outside the narrative. Although hearers will naturally question their fortitude in the face of opposition, they need not worry about God's faithfulness. Indeed, the opposition itself is, as an emulation of Jesus' own path, a sign of that faithfulness. In this sense the very promise of divine empowerment fosters obedience to the impossible discipleship task: Go and follow the path of Jesus, for God will be with you.

Notes

Introduction

1. *Phaedr.* 250a, trans. A. Nehmas and P. Woodruff (Indianapolis: Hackett, 1995); Quoted in Conor Cunningham, *Genealogy of Nihilism: Philosophies of Nothing and the Difference of Theology* (London: Routledge, 2002), 222.
2. See Elizabeth Struthers Malbon, "Disciples/Crowds/Whoever," in *In the Company of Jesus: Characters in Mark's Gospel* (Louisville: Westminster John Knox, 2000), 77–99; Robert Tannehill, "The Disciples in Mark: The Function of a Narrative Role," in *The Interpretation of Mark*, ed. William R. Telford (Edinburgh: T & T Clark, 1995), 171–72; and Ernest Best, "The Role of the Disciples in Mark," *New Testament Studies* 23 (1977): 380–81, 392–93.
3. Hans-Georg Gadamer, *Truth and Method*, 3rd ed., trans. and rev. Joel Weinsheimer and Donald G. Marshall (New York: Continuum, 1993), 375.
4. Nils Dahl, "The Neglected Factor in New Testament Theology," in *Jesus the Christ: The Historical Origins of Christological Doctrine*, ed. Donald H. Juel (Minneapolis: Fortress, 1991), 154.
5. For example, Ferdinand Hahn, "The Confession of the One God in the New Testament," *Horizons in Biblical Theology* 2 (1980): 69–84; Pheme Perkins, "God in the New Testament: Preliminary Soundings," *Theology Today* 42 (1985): 332–41; Jouette M. Bassler, "God (NT)," *Anchor Bible Dictionary*, ed. David Noel Freedman, 6 vols. (New York: Doubleday, 1992), 2:1049–55; Marianne Meye Thompson, *The Promise of the Father: Jesus and God in the New Testament* (Louisville: Westminster John Knox, 2000); A. Andrew Das and Frank J. Matera, eds., *The Forgotten God: Perspectives in Biblical Theology: Essays in Honor of Paul J. Achtemeier on the Occasion of His Seventy-fifth Birthday* (Louisville: Westminster John Knox, 2002). Recent scholarship has seen the emergence of studies, much like the present work, that focus on God in a particular biblical book. So W. Lee Humphreys, *The Character of God in the Book of Genesis: A Narrative Appraisal* (Louisville: Westminster John Knox, 2001); Marianne Meye Thompson, *The God of the Gospel of John* (Grand Rapids: Eerdmans, 2001). See also the survey of scholarship provided by Philip Reubin Johnson, "God in Mark: The Narrative Function of God as a Character in the Gospel of Mark" (PhD diss., Luther Seminary, 2000), 2–10.
6. John R. Donahue, "A Neglected Factor in the Theology of Mark," *Journal of Biblical Literature* 101 (1982): 562–94; idem, "The Revelation of God in the Gospel of Mark," in *Modern Biblical Scholarship: Its Impact on Theology and Proclamation*, ed. Francis A. Eigo (Villanova: Villanova University Press, 1984), 157–83; Donald H. Juel, *A Master of Surprise* (Minneapolis: Fortress, 1994);

idem, *The Gospel of Mark*, Interpreting Biblical Texts (Nashville: Abingdon, 1999); M. Eugene Boring, "Markan Christology: God-Language for Jesus?" *New Testament Studies* 45 (1999): 451–71; James S. Hanson, *The Endangered Promises: Conflict in Mark*, Society of Biblical Literature Dissertation Series 171 (Atlanta: Society of Biblical Literature, 2001); Paul L. Danove, "The Narrative Function of Mark's Characterization of God," *Novum Testamentum* 43 (2001): 12–30; idem, *The Rhetoric of Characterization of God, Jesus, and Jesus' Disciples in the Gospel of Mark*, Journal for the Study of the New Testament Supplement 290 (New York: T & T Clark, 2005), 28–55; Jack Dean Kingsbury, "'God' within the Narrative World of Mark," in *Forgotten God*, 75–88. Unpublished dissertations include Kisun No, "The Narrative Function of God in the Gospel of Mark" (PhD diss., Southern Baptist Theological Seminary, 1999); and Johnson, "God in Mark."

7. See the surveys in Janice Capel Anderson and Stephen D. Moore, "Introduction: The Lives of Mark," in *Mark and Method: New Approaches in Biblical Studies*, ed. Janice Capel Anderson and Stephen D. Moore (Minneapolis: Fortress, 1992), 1–21; and Norman Perrin, "The Interpretation of the Gospel of Mark," *Interpretation* 30 (1976): 115–24. On the shift inaugurated by narrative criticism, see Mark Allan Powell, *What Is Narrative Criticism?* (Minneapolis: Fortress, 1990), 1–10.

8. Dahl's examples are Acts 17:24–29; Rom. 1:18ff., 9:14ff.; John 4:24; and 1 John 1:5; 4:8 ("Neglected Factor," 156). This is also the tendency in Danove, "Mark's Characterization of God," passim; idem, *Rhetoric of Characterization*, passim.

9. Robert Fowler, *Let the Reader Understand: Reader-Response Criticism and the Gospel of Mark* (Minneapolis: Fortress, 1991).

10. Seymour Chatman, *Story and Discourse: Narrative Structure in Fiction and Film* (Ithaca: Cornell University Press, 1978), 19–42; Fowler, *Let the Reader Understand*, 2–3.

11. Fowler, *Let the Reader Understand*, 2.

12. Ibid., 15–16. Cf. Matt. 3:17. See also Jack Dean Kingsbury, *The Christology of Mark's Gospel* (Philadelphia: Fortress, 1983), 67; and Lamar Williamson Jr., *Mark*, Interpretation: A Bible Commentary for Teaching and Preaching (Atlanta: John Knox, 1983), 35.

13. I explore the fuller significance of this scene in chapter one.

14. See the discussion in Fowler, *Let the Reader Understand*, 10–14. Interpreters showing notable sensitivity to Mark's use of irony include Robert Fowler, *Loaves and Fishes: The Function of the Feeding Stories in the Gospel of Mark*, Society of Biblical Literature Dissertation Series 54 (Chico, CA: Scholars Press, 1981); Jerry Camery-Hoggatt, *Irony in Mark's Gospel: Text and Subtext*, Society for New Testament Studies Monograph Series 72 (Cambridge: Cambridge University Press, 1992); and Juel, *Master*.

15. Fowler, *Let the Reader Understand*, 42.

16. Stanley Fish, *Is There a Text in This Class? The Authority of Interpretive Communities* (Cambridge: Harvard University Press, 1980), 27.

17. That a reader may have encountered Mark's Gospel once or many times before would obviously result in somewhat different reading experiences, insofar as the reader would know beforehand her narrative path in its entirety. At the same time, however, I would not want to exaggerate these differences. In watching a particular movie for a second or third time, for instance, we will-

ingly surrender to the temporality of the story (assuming we do not fast-forward or rewind) and thereby reexperience the dynamic process of our initial viewing. I would argue that the same thing happens when we reread a story with which we are already familiar. Indeed, rereading may well bring to light certain dynamic moments along the narrative path that we had not noticed in previous reading. A rereading will never be identical to an initial reading, then, but neither will it be something altogether different. On the task of rereading see Patrick J. Wilson and Beverly Roberts Gaventa, "Preaching as the Re-reading of Scripture," *Interpretation* 52 (1998): 393–95.

18. Fish, *Is There a Text?* 37–40; see also Wolfgang Iser, *The Act of Reading: A Theory of Aesthetic Response* (Baltimore: Johns Hopkins University Press, 1978), 111.

19. Fowler, *Let the Reader Understand*, 42; see also J. L. Austin, *How to Do Things with Words* (Cambridge: Harvard University Press, 1962), 132–34; Walter Ong, *Orality and Literacy: The Technologizing of the Word* (London: Methuen, 1982), 8, 32–33, 76, 176–77; Eric A. Havelock, *The Literate Revolution in Greece and Its Cultural Consequences* (Princeton: Princeton University Press, 1982), 47–54; M. H. Abrams, *The Mirror and the Lamp: Romantic Theory and the Critical Tradition* (New York: Oxford University Press, 1953), 3–29; Peter M. Candler Jr., *Theology, Rhetoric, Manuduction, or Reading Scripture Together on the Path to God* (Grand Rapids: Eerdmans, 2006), 36–37; Jane P. Tompkins, "The Reader in History: The Changing Shape of Reader Response," in *Reader-Response Criticism: From Formalism to Post-Structuralism*, ed. Jane P. Tompkins (Baltimore: Johns Hopkins University Press, 1980), 201–32.

20. One should note that Jesus addresses not only the disciples but, more exactly, "those who were with him along with the disciples" (4:10). This implies that Mark does not identify the recipients of "the secret of the kingdom of God" (4:11) with the disciples, strictly speaking. Nevertheless, the mere inclusion of the disciples at 4:10 implies a contrast between the disciples and "those outside."

21. I explore the fuller significance of this scene in chapter three.

22. Powell, *What Is Narrative Criticism?* 19. See also Wayne C. Booth, *The Rhetoric of Fiction*, 2nd ed. (Chicago: University of Chicago Press, 1983), 151; Wolfgang Iser, *The Implied Reader: Patterns of Communication in Prose Fiction from Bunyan to Beckett* (Baltimore: Johns Hopkins University Press, 1974), xii; and Chatman, *Story and Discourse*, 147–53.

23. Identifying the original author and readers should be understood as a different matter than the larger historical context of, say, first-century Judaism, of which the New Testament represents only a small part of the evidence, and a knowledge of which will inform one's interpretation of the New Testament, including one's understanding of the historical author/audience. See David Rhoads, *Reading Mark: Engaging the Gospel* (Minneapolis: Fortress, 2004), 27–28.

24. So Mieke Bal, *Narratology: Introduction to the Theory of Narrative*, 2nd ed. (Toronto: University of Toronto Press, 1997), xiii.

25. See Whitney Shiner, *Proclaiming the Gospel: First-Century Performance of Mark* (Harrisburg: Trinity Press International, 2003); Harry Y. Gamble, *Books and Readers in the Early Church: A History of Early Christian Texts* (New Haven: Yale University Press, 1995), 211–24.

26. See Whitney Shiner, "Creating the Kingdom: The Performance of Mark as Revelatory Event," in *Literary Encounters with the Reign of God*, ed. Sharon H. Ringe and H. C. Paul Kim (New York: T & T Clark, 2004), 194–212; Gamble, *Books and Readers*, 204. See also Rhoads, *Reading Mark*, 176–201.

27. So Tannehill, "Disciples in Mark," 175–76, 178.
28. On the use of Scripture in Mark see Joel Marcus, *The Way of the Lord: Christological Exegesis of the Old Testament in the Gospel of Mark* (Louisville: Westminster John Knox, 1992); and Donald H. Juel, *Messianic Exegesis: Christological Interpretation of the Old Testament in Early Christianity* (Philadelphia: Fortress, 1988). On the early church's use of Scripture, see also Richard B. Hays, *Echoes of Scripture in the Letters of Paul* (New Haven: Yale University Press, 1989).
29. Jonathan Culler, "Literary Competence," in *Reader-Response Criticism*, 111.

Chapter One

1. On the distinction between character and actor see Shlomith Rimmon-Kenan, *Narrative Fiction: Contemporary Poetics* (London: Routledge, 1989), 34–36; Chatman, *Story and Discourse*, 107–45.
2. Although the phrase υἱοῦ θεοῦ at 1:1 is text-critically problematic, God directly names Jesus "Son" in v. 11 (see also 3:17; 5:7; 9:7; 12:6; 14:61–62; 15:39). On the text-critical issue see Bruce M. Metzger, *A Textual Commentary on the Greek New Testament*, 2nd ed. (Stuttgart: Deutsche Bibelgesellschaft, 1994), 62.
3. See Juel, *Messianic Exegesis*, 59–88, especially 77–81; Marcus, *Way of the Lord*, 59–72.
4. On the conflation of these scriptural verses see Marcus, *Way of the Lord*, 12–47.
5. See Juel, *Master*, 38–39; idem, *Mark*, 58–59.
6. The seeds for this tension were planted in Mark's use of the second person at 1:2 (προσώπου σου, ὁδόν σου), by which God's own announcement established a parallel between "the way of the Lord" and someone distinct from God ("before *you*," "*your* way"). In the case of the former Mark may have even changed a key phrase from Exod. 23:20 to fit this purpose. Cf. Mary Ann Tolbert, *Sowing the Gospel: Mark's World in Literary-Historical Perspective* (Minneapolis: Fortress, 1989), 239–48.
7. On the overlapping of theological and christological emphases in these verses see C. Clifton Black, "The Face Is Familiar—I Just Can't Place It," in *The Ending of Mark and the Ends of God: Essays in Memory of Donald Harrisville Juel*, ed. Beverly Roberts Gaventa and Patrick D. Miller (Louisville: Westminster John Knox, 2005), 36–38; Boring, "Markan Christology," 463–64; Tolbert, *Sowing the Gospel*, 240–41. The term κύριος will continue to refer to both Jesus (2:28; 5:19; 11:3) and God (11:9; 12:11, 29, 30; 13:20), and Jesus himself will exploit the ambiguity in a debate at 12:36–37.
8. Juel, *Master*, 39. See Matt. 3:14–15; Luke 3:18–22.
9. See P. J. Sankey, "Promise and Fulfilment: Reader-Response to Mark 1.1–15," *Journal for the Study of the New Testament* 58 (1995): 13–14; Robert G. Hamerton-Kelly, *The Gospel and the Sacred: Poetics of Violence in Mark* (Minneapolis: Fortress, 1994), 67.
10. Hamerton-Kelly, *Gospel and Sacred*, 69.
11. On the divine transcendence implied by God's and Jesus' speech about each other, see John R. Donahue, "Neglected Factor," passim.
12. Matt. 3:16; Luke 3:21.
13. So Juel, *Master*, 34–36. See Isa. 64:1; Ezek. 1:1; Rev. 4:1; Josephus, *Jewish War* 5.212–14. This interpretation is reinforced by the fact that Mark's only use of the verb σχίζω comes at 15:38—the tearing of the temple curtain at the moment of Jesus' death. See also David Ulansey, "The Heavenly Veil Torn: Mark's Cos-

mic *Inclusio*," *Journal of Biblical Literature* 110 (1991): 123–25; Daniel M. Gurtner, "LXX Syntax and the Identity of the NT Veil," *Novum Testamentum* 47
(2005): 344–53.

14. Juel, *Mark*, 61.

15. Ibid.

16. Juel, *Master*, 35–36.

17. It is worth acknowledging that Greek prepositions exhibit considerable fluidity
in meaning, such that one cannot simply assume the most common rendering
in every case. This is perhaps also a justification behind the NRSV translation
of εἰς as "upon" in Mark 1:10. It is clear, however, that when Mark wants to say
"on" or "upon" he uses the pronoun ἐπί—at least 28 times by my count (2:10,
21; 4:1, 5, 16, 20, 21, 26, 31[bis], 38; 6:25, 28, 39, 47, 48, 49, 53, 55; 7:30; 9:3,
20; 10:16; 11:2, 7; 13:2, 15; 14:35)—and not the preposition εἰς (which occurs
155 times in the narrative). So although statistics alone cannot make an argument for translation, they do strongly suggest, in this case, that God's Spirit
descends "into" Jesus.

18. Cf. Robert Tannehill, "The Gospel of Mark as Narrative Christology," *Semeia*
16 (1979): 63.

19. That this possession begins here should not be taken to imply an adoptionist
Christology, whereby God, precisely at that moment, chooses Jesus from
among other potential candidates. After all, the opening conflation of Malachi
and Isaiah locates Jesus within God's scriptural plan, so that the baptism merely
reveals the "Lord" whose way John has prepared. Jesus is not adopted but
promised. Concern for this potential misreading may have motivated the
scribal alteration to ἐπί in later manuscripts (see Marcus, *Mark 1–8*, 160).

20. Cf. Susan R. Garrett, *The Temptations of Jesus in Mark's Gospel* (Grand Rapids:
Eerdmans, 1998), 59.

21. Johnson, "God in Mark," 179. See also Danove, *Rhetoric of Characterization*, 51.

22. Defining "the" Markan prologue has been a matter of some debate. See Leander E. Keck, "The Introduction to Mark's Gospel," *New Testament Studies* 12
(1966): 352–70; Augustine Stock, "Hinge Transitions in Mark's Gospel," *Biblical Theology Bulletin* 15 (1985): 28; Tolbert, *Sowing the Gospel*, 108 n. 37.

23. Construing Ἰησοῦ Χριστοῦ ("of Jesus Christ") as an objective genitive construction. So Robert A. Guelich, *Mark 1–8:26*, Word Biblical Commentary
34A (Dallas: Word, 1989), 9; Morna Hooker, *The Gospel According to Saint
Mark*, Black's New Testament Commentaries (Peabody, MA: Hendrickson,
1991), 34; Charles Homer Giblin, "The Beginning of the Ongoing Gospel (Mk
1,2–16,8)," in *The Four Gospels 1992: Festschrift Frans Neirynck*, ed. F. Van Segbroeck et al., 3 vols., Bibliotheca ephemeridum theologicaium lovaniensium
100 (Leuven: Leuven University Press, 1992), 2:982–85. Cf. J. K. Elliott, "Mark
and the Teaching of Jesus: An Examination of ΛΟΓΟΣ and ΕΥΑΓΓΕΛΙΟΝ," in
Sayings of Jesus: Canonical and Non-canonical: Essays in Honor of Tjitze Baarda, ed.
William L. Petersen et al., Novum Testamentum Supplement 89 (Leiden: Brill,
1997), 43–44.

24. Construing Ἰησοῦ Χριστοῦ ("of Jesus Christ") as a subjective genitive construction. So Hugh Anderson, *The Gospel of Mark*, New Century Bible Commentary (1976; repr. Grand Rapids: Eerdmans, 1981), 67.

25. Iser, *Act of Reading*, 111.

26. See the summary in Brian K. Blount, *Go Preach! Mark's Kingdom Message and
the Black Church Today* (Maryknoll, NY: Orbis, 1998), 85 n. 5. An insightful

exception is Joel Marcus, *Mark 1–8*, Anchor Bible 27 (New York: Doubleday, 2000), 146–47.

27. Blount, *Go Preach!* 86.
28. Cf. Mark 9:35; Matt. 3:17.
29. So Jean Delorme, "Text and Context: 'The Gospel' According to Mark 1:14–18," in *Text and Logos: The Humanistic Interpretation of the New Testament*, ed. Theodore W. Jennings Jr. (Atlanta: Scholars Press, 1990), 281–82. Cf. Frank Matera, "The Prologue as the Interpretive Key to Mark's Gospel," *Journal for the Study of the New Testament* 34 (1988): 5–6.
30. Blount, *Go Preach!* 16, 83–92. See also James G. Williams, *Gospel against Parable: Mark's Language of Mystery*, Bible and Literature Series 12 (Sheffield: Almond, 1985), 92–97, 138.
31. Hanson, *Endangered Promises*, 123.
32. Ibid., 137; see also Ulrich Mauser, *Christ in the Wilderness: The Wilderness Theme in the Second Gospel and Its Basis in the Biblical Tradition*, Studies in Biblical Theology 1/39 (London: SCM, 1963), 82.
33. Mark's two other references to the "beloved Son" strengthen this ominous tone. First, at Jesus' transfiguration God's own command to heed "my beloved Son" (9:7) falls between Jesus' first two passion predictions (8:31; 9:31). Second, within the parable of the Wicked Tenants Jesus refers to himself as the "beloved Son" who will be beaten and killed (12:6–7). See Sharyn Dowd and Elizabeth Struthers Malbon, "The Significance of Jesus' Death in Mark: Narrative Context and Authorial Audience," *Journal of Biblical Literature* 125 (2006): 273–74.
34. Nils Dahl has discerned this very dynamic in the larger canonical story in "The Crucified Messiah and the Endangered Promises," in *Jesus the Christ*, 65–79. Dahl's essay marks the theological starting point for Hanson's treatment of Mark.
35. Hanson, *Endangered Promises*, 120. Some have argued that Mark's Gospel was even intended for a baptismal setting, e.g., Robin Scroggs and Kent I. Groff, "Baptism in Mark: Dying and Rising with Christ," *Journal of Biblical Literature* 92 (1973): 531–48; see also Marcus, *Mark 1–8*, 158, 170, 174–76, 221–22, 367, 369, 384, 475, 479.
36. Hanson, *Endangered Promises*, 133.
37. Dan O. Via Jr., *The Ethics of Mark's Gospel: In the Middle of Time* (Philadelphia: Fortress, 1985), 40–59. See also Williams, *Gospel Against Parable*, 97, 138.

Chapter Two

1. Jerome, *Tract. Marc.* 2.100–101.
2. For example, in order of publication, Anderson, *Gospel of Mark*, 86; John Reumann, "Mark 1:14–20," *Interpretation* 32 (1978): 405–10; Ernest Best, *Following Jesus: Discipleship in the Gospel of Mark*, Journal for the Study of the New Testament Supplement 4 (Sheffield: JSOT Press, 1981), 169; John R. Donahue, *The Theology and Setting of Discipleship in the Gospel of Mark* (Milwaukee: Marquette University Press, 1983), 14–15; Williamson, *Mark*, 45–48; Samuel O. Abogunrin, "The Three Variant Accounts of Peter's Call: A Critical and Theological Examination of the Texts," *New Testament Studies* 31 (1985): 590; Demetrios Trakatellis, "Ἀκολούθει μοι/Follow me' (Mk 2.14): Discipleship and Priesthood," *Greek Orthodox Theological Review* 30 (1985): 272–74; Paul J. Achtemeier, *Mark*, 2nd ed., Proclamation Commentaries (Philadelphia: Fortress,

1986), 47; John Christopher Thomas, "Discipleship in Mark's Gospel," in *Faces of Renewal: Studies in Honor of Stanley M. Horton Presented on His 70th Birthday*, ed. Paul Elbert (Peabody, MA: Hendrickson, 1988), 60, 68–69; Jack Dean Kingsbury, *Conflict in Mark: Jesus, Authorities, Disciples* (Minneapolis: Fortress, 1989), 90; Guelich, *Mark 1–8:26*, 53; Christopher D. Marshall, *Faith as a Theme in Mark's Narrative*, Society for New Testament Studies Monograph Series 64 (Cambridge: Cambridge University Press, 1989), 136–39; Donald English, *The Message of Mark* (Downers Grove, IL: InterVarsity Press, 1992), 52; Blount, *Go Preach!* 87; Marcus, *Mark 1–8*, 182; James R. Edwards, *The Gospel According to Mark*, Pillar New Testament Commentary (Grand Rapids: Eerdmans, 2002), 50; Johnson, "God in Mark," 236; Francis J. Moloney, *The Gospel of Mark: A Commentary* (Peabody, MA: Hendrickson, 2002), 53.

3. I presuppose the two-source hypothesis, whereby Matthew and Luke are believed to have used Mark and the hypothetical "Q" as the major sources for composing their own Gospels. See M. É. Boismard, "Two-Source Hypothesis," *Anchor Bible Dictionary* 6:679–82.

4. Chatman, *Story and Discourse*, 45–46.

5. Jerome, *Tract. Marc.* 9.37–44 (Corpus Christianorum: Series latina 78:492).

6. Although Mark describes two distinct encounters (1:16–18, 19–20), I take the former, with its description of Jesus' summons (1:17), as paradigmatic.

7. Contra, e.g., Marshall, *Faith as a Theme*, 137; Reumann, "Mark 1:14–20."

8. So Whitney Taylor Shiner, *Follow Me! Disciples in Markan Rhetoric*, Society of Biblical Literature Dissertation Series 145 (Atlanta: Scholars Press, 1995), 183; J. Duncan M. Derrett, "'Ησαν γαρ 'αλιεισ (Mk. i 16): Jesus's Fishermen and the Parable of the Net," *Novum Testamentum* 22 (1980): 112–13.

9. Shiner, *Follow Me!* 188; see also Best, *Following Jesus*, 137.

10. See also Shiner, *Follow Me!* 188.

11. Jerome, *Tract. Marc.* 2.125–27.

12. Exod. 13:18, 20; 14:3, 11, 12; 15:22; 16:1, 3, 10, 14, 32; 17:1; 18:5; 19:1, 2.

13. Marcus, *Mark 1–8*, 151. See Exod. 13:4, 8; Deut. 23:5; Josh. 2:10.

14. Josh. 24:5, 17; Judg. 2:1, 12; 6:7–10, 13; 1 Sam. 10:18; 1 Kgs. 8:16, 21 (= 2 Chr. 6:10); 8:51, 53; 9:9 (= 2 Chr. 7:22); 2 Kgs. 17:7, 36; Pss. 77:52–55; 80:11; 104:37, 43; 105:10, 47; 135:11, 16; Jer. 2:6–7; 7:22; 11:3–5, 7; 39:21; 41:13; Ezek. 20:6, 9; Dan. 9:15; Hos. 12:14; Amos 2:10; 3:1; 9:7; Mic. 6:4. The exodus out of Egypt also marks the "birth" or "election" of Israel in Exod. 4:22; Jer. 2:2–3; and Hos. 11:1. See also Deut. 32:10 and Ezek. 20:5. See Mauser, *Christ in the Wilderness*, 27–29.

15. The exceptions are 1 Kgs. 8:16, 21 (= 2 Chr. 6:10); Pss. 104: 37, 43; 135:11, 16.

16. See Elizabeth Struthers Malbon, "Texts and Contexts: Interpreting the Disciples in Mark," in *Company of Jesus*, 100–130.

17. James M. Robinson, *The Problem of History in Mark*, Studies in Biblical Theology 1/21 (Naperville, IL: Allenson, 1957), 24.

18. Contra Danove: "the context presents no warrants explaining Jesus' authority to make such an invitation" (*Rhetoric of Characterization*, 19).

19. So Boring, "Markan Christology," 466.

20. See also Mark 7:29–30, 34–35; 9:25–26; 11:12–14, 20–25.

21. "Quia sermo ipse Domini operatorius erat: et quodcumque dicebat, opere efficiebat" (Jerome, *Tract. Marc.* 2.131–32).

22. Williamson, *Mark*, 45; see also Abogunrin, "Three Variant Accounts," 590.

23. Anderson, *Gospel of Mark*, 87–88.

24. Eduard Schweizer, *The Good News According to Mark*, trans. Donald H. Madvig (Atlanta: John Knox, 1970), 48 (my emphasis).

25. Eduard Schweizer, "The Portrayal of the Life of Faith in the Gospel of Mark," *Interpretation* 32 (1978): 395–96.

26. Marcus, *Mark 1–8*, 181. See also Charles W. F. Smith, "Fishers of Men: Footnotes on a Gospel Figure," *Harvard Theological Review* 52 (1959): 191; Boring, "Markan Christology," 465.

27. Marcus, *Mark 1–8*, 185.

28. Blount, *Go Preach!* 8. See also Robinson, *The Problem of History*, 47; Via, *Ethics of Mark's Gospel*, 61–63.

29. See Smith, "Fishers of Men," 187–88; Wilhelm H. Wuellner, *The Meaning of "Fishers of Men,"* New Testament Library (Philadelphia: Westminster, 1967), 88–107, 126–31.

30. Four of these references (Job 19:6; Isa. 37:29; Ezek. 38:4; Amos 4:2) have been either omitted or altered in the LXX. See also Matt. 13:47–50.

31. Cf. Derrett, "'Ησαν γαρ 'αλιεισ," 117–19. For potential parallels outside Scripture see Marcus, *Mark 1–8*, 184–85; Wuellner, *Meaning of "Fishers of Men,"* 64–133.

32. Kingsbury, *Conflict in Mark*, 91. See also Hooker, *Saint Mark*, 60; Guelich, *Mark 1–8:26*, 51; Derrett, "'Ησαν γαρ 'αλιεισ," 108–21.

33. John R. Donahue, S.J., and Daniel J. Harrington, S.J., *The Gospel of Mark*, Sacra pagina (Collegeville, MN: Liturgical Press, 2002), 74. See also Best, *Following Jesus*, 170.

34. Tannehill, "Narrative Christology," 65.

35. The parallels are particularly pronounced in descriptions of "the twelve" at Mark 3:14b–15 (they are appointed to proclaim and have authority to cast out demons), 6:7b (they are given authority over unclean spirits), 6:12b (they proclaim a message of repentance), and 6:13a (they cast out many demons). Jesus provides the model for these activities at 1:14–15, 23–27, 34, 38–39; 3:11, 20–30; 5:2, 13; 7:24–30; 9:14–27; 11:27–33; 13:34.

36. Blount, *Go Preach!* 102–3.

37. Tannehill, "Narrative Christology," 64.

38. Hanson, *Endangered Promises*, 236. See also Juel, *Master*, 63.

39. So Hanson, *Endangered Promises*, 224.

40. Via, *Ethics of Mark's Gospel*, 40–59.

41. Juel, *Mark*, 76.

Chapter Three

1. Frank Kermode, *The Genesis of Secrecy: On the Interpretation of Narrative* (Cambridge: Harvard University Press, 1979), 27.

2. On the history of interpretation regarding the disciples in Mark, see the discussion in Hanson, *Endangered Promises*, 211–20. See also Frank J. Matera, *What Are They Saying about Mark?* (New York: Paulist Press, 1987), 38–55.

3. Kermode, *Genesis of Secrecy*, 27.

4. I add this qualification because the troubling characterization of the disciples within the narrative will presumably give way to their restoration beyond the end of the narrative (13:9–13), thus fully realizing Jesus' promise at 1:17. See chapter five.

5. Such a "break" seems not to entail an absolute and permanent severing of all former ties, as seen by the subsequent episode at Peter's own house (1:29–34),

as well as the disciples' continued access to boats (3:9; 4:1, 35–41; 5:18; 6:45, 47–52; 8:10). See Rhoads, *Reading Mark*, 105.

6. Tannehill, "Narrative Christology," 68.

7. I use the word "crowds" to refer to the multitudes that flock to Jesus, even in those scenes where the noun ὄχλος does not appear (e.g., 1:21–28, 32–34). Mark refers specifically to the ὄχλος at 2:4, 13; 3:9, 20, 32; 4:1, 36; 5:21, 24, 27, 30, 31; 6:34, 45; 7:14, 17, 33; 8:1, 2, 6, 34; 9:14, 15, 17, 25; 10:1, 46; 11:18, 32; 12:12, 37, 41; 14:43; 15:8, 11, 15. On the fluidity between "disciples" and "crowds" see Malbon, *Company of Jesus*, 75–78.

8. Even for those characters who exhibit "faith," the attraction to Jesus seems simply to be Jesus' power to heal in the context of his extremely popular ministry, not the specific issue of Jesus as agent of God's eschatological reign (2:5; 5:34, 36; 9:23–24; 10:52). So Rhoads, *Reading Mark*, 81–82. At 2:12 bystanders do glorify God in response to Jesus' healing of the paralytic, but this response is coupled, somewhat negatively, with amazement (cf. 3:21; 5:42; 6:51), thus accentuating the cognitive distance between the dumbfounded characters, with their limited perspective, and the knowledgeable audience, privileged from the beginning by Mark's discourse. See Jonathan Bishop, "*Parabole* and *Parrhesia* in Mark," *Interpretation* 40 (1986): 44. Cf. Marshall, *Faith as a Theme*, 75–133.

9. On the literary and rhetorical coherence of this unit within the larger narrative, see Joanna Dewey, "The Literary Structure of the Controversy Stories in Mark 2:1–3:6," in *Interpretation of Mark*, 141–51; idem, *Markan Public Debate: Literary Technique, Concentric Structure, and Theology in Mark 2:1–3:6*, Society of Biblical Literature Dissertation Series 48 (Chico, CA: Scholars Press, 1980); Joseph Keller, "Jesus and the Critics: A Logo-Critical Analysis of the Marcan Confrontation," *Interpretation* 40 (1986): 34.

10. Although the "leaders," as I call them, carry various titles (Pharisees, scribes, priests, elders, Sadducees) and express some distinctive concerns, I follow the majority of narrative critics who treat them as a relatively coherent character group, particularly by virtue of their shared opposition to Jesus and the implicit threat Jesus represents to them. See Malbon, "The Jewish Leaders in the Gospel of Mark: A Literary Study of Markan Characterization," in *Company of Jesus*, 149–52; Kingsbury, *Conflict in Mark*, 14, 64–65; Hanson, *Endangered Promises*, 196; David Rhoads, Joanna Dewey, and Donald Michie, *Mark as Story: An Introduction to the Narrative of a Gospel*, 2nd ed. (Minneapolis: Fortress, 1999), 116.

11. So Tannehill, "Disciples in Mark," 181; contra Tolbert, *Sowing the Gospel*, 141–42.

12. Suzanne Watts Henderson, "'Concerning the Loaves': Comprehending Incomprehension in Mark 6:45–52," *Journal for the Study of the New Testament* 83 (2001): 15. See also Thomas, "Discipleship in Mark's Gospel," 70–71.

13. Ched Myers, *Binding the Strong Man: A Political Reading of Mark's Story of Jesus* (Maryknoll, NY: Orbis, 1997), 163.

14. See Dowd and Malbon, "Significance of Jesus' Death," 276.

15. See Blount, *Go Preach!* 99–111; Juel, *Master*, 65–75; Robinson, *Problem of History*, 38.

16. Juel, *Mark*, 59.

17. Ibid., 64.

18. Following Juel, *Master*, 45–63. Cf. Williams, *Gospel Against Parable*, 87–88.

19. Marcus, *Mark 1–8*, 295.

20. Juel, *Master*, 57.

21. See especially Mark 4:26–29 (Marcus, *Mark 1–8*, 328); 13:20, 24–37.
22. See Juel, *Master*, 48–50; Marcus, *Mark 1–8*, 305–6; and the more extensive survey in Mary Ann Beavis, *Mark's Audience: The Literary and Social Setting of Mark 4:11–12*, Journal for the Study of the New Testament Supplement 33 (Sheffield: Sheffield Academic Press, 1989), 69–86. This tendency goes all the way back to the redaction of Mark at Matt. 13:13.
23. On the thematic parallels to Isaiah see Craig A. Evans, "A Note on the Function of Isaiah, VI 9–10 in Mark, IV," *Revue biblique* 88 (1981): 234–35; idem, "On the Isaianic Background of the Sower Parable," *Catholic Biblical Quarterly* 47 (1985): 464–68; Marcus, *Mark 1–8*, 298–307.
24. Juel, *Master*, 49. See also Marcus, *Mark 1–8*, 299–300.
25. See Greg Fay, "Introduction to Incomprehension: The Literary Structure of Mark 4:1–34," *Catholic Biblical Quarterly* 51 (1989): 65–73.
26. Michael D. Goulder, "Those Outside (Mk. 4:10–12)," *Novum Testamentum* 33 (1991): 289.
27. For example, Mark 1:44; 5:43; 7:36; 8:26; 9:9.
28. For example, Mark 4:10–34; 8:14–21, 27–33; 9:11–13, 30–37; 10:32–46; 11:20–25; 13:1–37; 14:22–31.
29. Cf. Tolbert, *Sowing the Gospel*, 160.
30. Juel, *Master*, 58.
31. Shiner, *Follow Me!* 207.
32. On the parallels to this theme in Jewish apocalyptic literature, see Joel Marcus, "Mark 4:10–12 and Marcan Epistemology," *Journal of Biblical Literature* 103 (1984): 557–74.
33. Elizabeth Struthers Malbon, "Echoes and Foreshadowings in Mark 4–8: Reading and Rereading," *Journal of Biblical Literature* 112 (1993): 219. See also Marcus, *Mark 1–8*, 305.
34. Shiner, *Follow Me!* 211.
35. Hamerton-Kelly, *Gospel and Sacred*, 92.
36. A possible allusion to Jesus' godlike sovereignty, based on Near Eastern parallels (Marcus, *Mark 1–8*, 338).
37. Mitzi Minor, *The Spirituality of Mark: Responding to God* (Louisville: Westminster John Knox, 1996), 42.
38. Following the NRSV. The ambiguity of Mark's pronoun (αὐτὸν, "him") raises the question of who exactly is being asked to leave: Jesus or the former demoniac. In either interpretation, however, one sees the hostility toward God's transformative reign.
39. See Blount, *Go Preach!* 99–111; Hamerton-Kelly, *Gospel and Sacred*, 93.
40. The reference to Jairus's fear (φοβέομαι, 5:36) echoes 4:41 most precisely: "And they [the disciples] feared greatly" (ἐφοβήθησαν φόβον μέγαν). The first reference to the disciples' fear at 4:40 uses a different Greek term, δειλός.
41. Indeed, the people of Nazareth seem, unknowingly, to take offense at God and not just Jesus, in that God is the implied answer to their question, "From where did he get all this?" (Johnson, "God in Mark," 217–18).
42. I take this to mean simply that the scandalized Nazarene community, true to the scriptural pattern of prophet rejection, did not flock to Jesus as other communities did (1:32–39; 2:7–12; 5:24). It need not mean, in other words, that the people's disbelief suddenly rendered Jesus powerless as a healer. This would assume that one's faith could literally heal, a dynamic absent even at Mark 5:34 ("Daughter, your faith has healed you"), in that Mark there clarifies Jesus'

"power" (δύναμις, 5:30) as the actual healing agent. Thus the woman's "faith" consists in her bold and trusting movement toward Jesus in the desperate hope of healing, a healing she already knows is possible based on the fact that she had previously heard of Jesus (5:27). It is faith like this that is lacking in Nazareth, with the result that Jesus does not dwell there for long (6:6).

43. Although the term at 3:14 may be an interpolation (Marcus, *Mark 1–8*, 263; Metzger, *Textual Commentary*, 69), it is obviously the same group.

44. See Chatman, *Story and Discourse*, 63; Gérard Genette, *Narrative Discourse: An Essay in Method*, trans. Jane E. Lewin (Ithaca: Cornell University Press, 1980), 86–112.

45. Fowler, *Let the Reader Understand*, 216.

46. Mark 8:34–38; 9:33–37; 10:28–31, 41–45.

47. See also Mark 9:11–13.

48. See Exod. 16:13–35; Num. 11:1–35; Neh. 9:15; Ps. 78:17–31; Isa. 49:8–13.

49. See Henderson, "Concerning the Loaves," 13; Hanson, *Endangered Promises*, 232.

50. So Tannehill, "Disciples in Mark," 183. The irony of the two feeding stories has been treated extensively by Fowler, *Loaves and Fishes*, 43–100.

51. ASV, KJV, NAB, NIV, NKJV, NRSV, RSV.

52. See Exod. 3:13–15; Isa. 41:4; 43:10–11.

53. See Andrew T. Lincoln, "The Promise and the Failure: Mark 16:7, 8," *Journal of Biblical Literature* 108 (1989): 286–87.

54. Mark does not really explain what the disciples fail to understand "about the loaves." See, however, Henderson, "Concerning the Loaves," 12–25; Quentin Quesnell, *The Mind of Mark: Interpretation and Method through the Exegesis of Mark 6, 52* (Rome: Pontifical Biblical Institute Press, 1969), 58–67.

55. So Marcus, *Mark 1–8*, 427–28.

56. Ibid. See especially Exod. 4:21; 7:3; 9:12; 10:1, 20, 27; 11:10; 14:4, 8, 17. Connections to the book of Job are discerned by Adela Yarbro Collins, "Rulers, Divine Men, and Walking on the Water (Mark 6:45–52)," in *Religious Propaganda and Missionary Competition in the New Testament World: Essays Honoring Dieter Georgi*, ed. Lukas Bormann, Kelly Del Tredici, and Angela Standhartinger (Leiden: Brill, 1994), 226–27.

57. Henderson, "Concerning the Loaves," 5.

58. Note that Matthew alleviates the tension by omitting the reference to hardening altogether (Matt. 14:22–33).

59. See Fowler, *Loaves and Fishes*, passim; cf. L. Countryman, "How Many Baskets Full? Mark 8:14–21 and the Value of Miracles in Mark," *Catholic Biblical Quarterly* 47 (1985): 643–55.

60. Without factoring in the previous reference to divine hardening (6:52) one can only attribute such confusion to ineptitude and therefore blame the disciples outright (e.g., Tannehill, "Disciples in Mark," 183; Fowler, *Loaves and Fishes*, 104).

61. For example, Edwards, *Gospel According to Mark*, 240; Hanson, *Endangered Promises*, 235; Jeffrey B. Gibson, "The Rebuke of the Disciples in Mark 8:14–21," *Journal for the Study of the New Testament* 27 (1986): 33.

62. For example, Garrett, *Temptations*, 235.

63. As acknowledged by Garrett, *Temptations*, 56, 59.

64. See Norman Petersen, "Point of View in Mark's Narrative," *Semeia* 12 (1978): 107; Joanna Dewey, "Point of View and the Disciples in Mark," *Society*

of Biblical Literature Seminar Papers, 21 (Missoula, MT: Scholars Press, 1982), 97–106.

65. That 4:11–12 and 8:18 draw from different Scriptures (Isa. 6:9–10 and Jer. 5:21, respectively) does not take away from their obvious parallels to each other within the narrative, i.e., as the Markan audience would actually hear them (contra Hanson, *Endangered Promises*, 235).

66. Kevin Madigan, "Ancient and High-Medieval Interpretations of Jesus in Gethsemane: Some Reflections on Tradition and Continuity in Christian Thought," *Harvard Theological Review* 88 (1995): 160.

67. So Johnson, "God in Mark," 344.

68. See also Danove, *Rhetoric of Characterization*, 66.

69. Rhoads, Dewey, and Michie, *Mark as Story*, 103.

70. Tannehill, "Disciples in Mark," 184.

71. Ibid., 182.

72. Hanson, *Endangered Promises*, 235.

73. Rhoads, *Reading Mark*, 122.

74. In all ten passages the LXX uses the same verb: σκληρύνω. In the MT, Exod. 7:3 uses the verb קשׁה, Exod. 10:1 uses the verb כבד, while the remaining eight passages use the verb חזק. In addition to these, five passages (Exod. 7:13, 22; 8:19; 9:7, 35) make the more ambiguous statement that Pharaoh's heart simply "was hardened," though I would construe this as a divine passive.

75. Interestingly, the LXX employs a different verb (βαρύνω) in describing Pharaoh's hardening of his own heart; the MT uses כבד in all three passages. In the case of Exod. 8:15, the LXX changes the verb to the passive voice (ἐβαρύνθη ἡ καρδία αὐτοῦ), leaving the subject of the activity more ambiguous vis-à-vis the opening clause, where Pharaoh is clearly the subject (ἰδὼν δὲ Φαραὼ ὅτι γέγονεν ἀνάψυξις).

76. See Terence E. Fretheim, *Exodus*, Interpretation: A Bible Commentary for Teaching and Preaching (Louisville: John Knox, 1991), 96–103.

77. Garrett, *Temptations*, 75. This is precisely the assumption that leads Garrett to posit Satan, rather than God, as the hardening agent.

Chapter Four

1. Nick Cave, introduction to *The Gospel According to Mark* (Edinburgh: Canongate, 1998), xi.

2. See Juel, *Mark*, 163–65; Blount, *Go Preach!* 126–42; Tolbert, *Sowing the Gospel*, 262; Myers, *Binding*, 244; Minor, *Spirituality*, 55; David J. Lull, "Interpreting Mark's Story of Jesus' Death: Toward a Theology of Suffering," *Society of Biblical Literature Seminar Papers*, 24 (Atlanta: Scholars Press, 1985), 5–6.

3. After 8:17 the audience will never again hear of God's hardening activity. This does not mean, however, that previous references will not continue to exert a certain theological effect, for God's hardening now belongs to the audience's narrative memory and can resonate, to varying degrees, for the remainder of its journey.

4. I say "fully" surface because Jesus does provide a rather elliptical allusion at 2:20.

5. See Joel Marcus, "A Note on Markan Optics," *New Testament Studies* 45 (1999): 250–56.

6. Minor, *Spirituality*, 58. See also Garrett, *Temptations*, 79; Moloney, *Mark*, 167.

7. A fact that may have motivated Matthew's redaction of this verse: "And Jesus answered him, 'Blessed are you, Simon son of Jonah! For flesh and blood has not revealed this to you, but my Father in heaven'" (Matt. 16:17).

8. See Garrett, *Temptations*, 76–77. Peter is not literally the *character* Satan, or even literally possessed by a demon, since Jesus has proven perfectly capable of casting them out of people (Johnson, "God in Mark," 225–26). Scholarly obsession with the Satan reference unfortunately detracts from what I deem the more central issue, namely, the implied opposition between "the things of God" and "the things of humans" as it pertains to Jesus' passion. So Boring, "Markan Christology," 459.

9. James H. Charlesworth, "From Messianology to Christology: Problems and Prospects," in *The Messiah: Developments in Earliest Judaism and Christianity*, ed. James H. Charlesworth (Minneapolis: Fortress, 1992), 35. See also John J. Collins, *The Scepter and the Star: The Messiahs of the Dead Sea Scrolls and Other Ancient Literature* (New York: Doubleday, 1995); Marinus de Jonge, "Messiah," *Anchor Bible Dictionary*, 4:777–88.

10. Charlesworth, "From Messianology to Christology," 33 (my emphasis). Charlesworth provides a helpful survey of the diversity of beliefs and expectations, a diversity unanimously recognized by the 1987 Princeton Symposium on Judaism and Christian Origins (Charlesworth, "Preface," in *Messiah*, xv).

11. The disjunction applies equally to the designation "Son of Man," if Mark means it as a kind of title drawn from the book of Daniel (8:31; see also 2:10, 28; 8:38; 9:9, 12, 31; 10:33, 45; 13:26; 14:21, 41, 62). See Roy A. Harrisville, *Fracture: The Cross as Irreconcilable in the Language and Thought of the Biblical Writers* (Grand Rapids: Eerdmans, 2006), 134–35.

12. Matthew L. Skinner, "Denying Self, Bearing a Cross, and Following Jesus: Unpacking the Imperatives of Mark 8:34," *Word and World* 23 (2003): 324.

13. The same psalm refers to the royal "son" as God's "anointed" (Ps. 2:2).

14. Following Juel, *Master*, 96. See also Bishop, "*Parabole* and *Parrhesia*," 51. On the experience of such mockery through oral performance, see Shiner, "Creating the Kingdom," 203–4.

15. Juel, *Master*, 97. See also Shiner, *Follow Me!* 262.

16. See Minor, *Spirituality*, 59; Shiner, *Follow Me!* 275. Cf. James L. Mays, "Exposition of Mark 8:27–9:1," *Interpretation* 30 (1976): 176.

17. Johnson, "God in Mark," 245.

18. NRSV: "that the Son of Man *must* undergo great suffering" (8:31).

19. See Harrisville, *Fracture*, 132.

20. Although Jesus' counterrebuke uses a second-person singular verb (in response to Peter), he implicates the whole group by "turning and looking at his disciples" while he speaks (8:33).

21. The parallels have been treated more extensively by Hanson, *Endangered Promises*, 229–36.

22. So Johnson, "God in Mark," 234; Minor, *Spirituality*, 25–33.

23. The potential allusions to Isaac's binding via the designation "beloved" (1:11; 9:7), along with Jesus' earlier reference to the bridegroom being "taken away" (ἀπαρθῇ, 2:20; divine passive?), may suggest divine agency; but they do not specify divine necessity. See Dowd and Malbon, "Significance of Jesus' Death," 273–76.

24. This is also the dynamic implied by Mark's account of the death of John the Baptist (6:17–29).

25. On "the way" see Williams, *Gospel Against Parable*, 100–104.
26. Dowd and Malbon, "Significance of Jesus' Death," 281–82. See also Skinner, "Denying Self," passim; Joanna Dewey, "'Let Them Renounce Themselves and Take Up Their Cross': A Feminist Reading of Mark 8:34 in Mark's Social and Narrative World," in *A Feminist Companion to Mark*, ed. Amy-Jill Levine (Cleveland: Pilgrim Press, 2001), 23–36.
27. See especially Norman Perrin, "Towards an Interpretation of the Gospel of Mark," in *Christology and a Modern Pilgrimage: A Discussion with Norman Perrin*, ed. Hans Dieter Betz (Claremont: New Testament Colloquium, 1971), 1–78.
28. Cf. Matt. 16:22. See Joseph B. Tyson, "The Blindness of the Disciples in Mark," *Journal of Biblical Literature* 80 (1961): 261–62. In addition to the instances of misunderstanding listed above, see also Mark 9:38–41; 10:13–16, 23–31.
29. Kingsbury, "God," 81.
30. For example, the resurrection, which is also included in the passion predictions (see Mark 9:9).
31. So Garrett, *Temptations*, 82–85.
32. On the common ideological ground shared by all the leadership groups see Hanson, *Endangered Promises*, 151–207. On the possible historical connections among them see Richard A. Horsley, *Hearing the Whole Story: The Politics of Plot in Mark's Gospel* (Louisville: Westminster John Knox, 2001), 149–76.
33. Interestingly, with the completion of the three passion predictions, Jesus' authority as prophet takes center stage, beginning with the preparations he makes for entering Jerusalem (11:1–10) and then moving to his parabolic indictment of the temple establishment (11:12–12:12; 12:38–44), his extensive eschatological speech (13:1–37), his preparations for the Passover meal (14:12–16), and his own predictions during the meal itself (14:17–31).
34. See Ira Brent Driggers, "The Politics of Divine Presence: Temple as Locus of Conflict in the Gospel of Mark," 17–28 (forthcoming in *Biblical Interpretation: A Journal of Contemporary Approaches* 15 [2007]: 270–90); Myers, *Binding the Strong Man*, 297–306.
35. Mark's depiction of the temple condemnation may draw from distinctively messianic traditions. See Donald Juel, *Messiah and Temple: The Trial of Jesus in the Gospel of Mark*, Society of Biblical Literature Dissertation Series 31 (Missoula, MT: Scholars Press, 1977), 117–97; James D. G. Dunn, "'Are You the Messiah?': Is the Crux of Mark 14:61–62 Resolvable?" in *Christology, Controversy and Community: New Testament Essays in Honour of David R. Catchpole*, ed. David G. Horrell and Christopher M. Tuckett, Novum Testamentum Supplement 99 (Leiden: Brill, 2000), 7–10.
36. Acknowledging its ambiguity, I am inclined to identify "the others" at 12:19 either with anyone (Jewish or Gentile) targeted by Jesus' ministry or the Twelve, who, as new tenants, are commissioned to extend Jesus' ministry to Jews and Gentiles alike. I do not think Mark's Gospel requires us to choose between a Gentile or Jewish referent, as assumed respectively by Joel Marcus, *Way of the Lord*, 115–28; and Aaron A. Milavec, "Mark's Parable of the Wicked Husbandmen as Reaffirming God's Predilection for Israel," *Journal of Ecumenical Studies* 26 (1989): 305–7, 311.
37. No, "Narrative Function of God," 131; see also Johnson, "God in Mark," 325–27.
38. The verb occurs in only these two instances.
39. See Tolbert, *Sowing the Gospel*, 92–106. A more thorough treatment may be found in Bal, *Narratology*, 43–75.

40. See Hamerton-Kelly, *Gospel and Sacred*, 34.
41. See Harrisville, *Fracture*, 133.
42. 3:31–35; 8:34–38; 9:35–37; 10:43–45.
43. C. Clifton Black, *The Rhetoric of the Gospel: Theological Artistry in the Gospels and Acts* (St. Louis: Chalice, 2001), 57. See also the direct address to the public reader at 13:14 (following Gamble, *Books and Readers*, 205–8; Donahue and Harrington, *Gospel of Mark*, 372; cf. Fowler, *Let the Reader Understand*, 83–85).
44. So Theodore J. Weeden, "Heresy," 94–95.
45. Black, *Rhetoric*, 53.
46. The exception to this is Mark 14:27 (cf. 16:7), Jesus' promise of restoration.
47. So Rhoads, Dewey, and Michie, *Mark as Story*, 47.
48. Hamerton-Kelly, *Gospel and Sacred*, 42.
49. I am inclined to explain Judas's motivation with reference to the intercalation of his betrayal (14:1–2, 10–11) with the episode of Jesus' anointing by an unnamed woman (14:3–9), an approach yielding two possibilities. Either Judas objects to Jesus' seemingly dismissive attitude toward the poor (14:7); or, finally realizing the nearness of Jesus' death (since Jesus describes the anointing as a preparation for his death), he cuts a deal to ensure the saving of his own hide (8:35; cf. Matt. 26:15; Luke 22:3).
50. See Marcus, *Way of the Lord*, 173.
51. This also affirms the tension inherent in Mark's ambiguous references to being "handed over" (παραδίδωμι), with respect not only to Jesus (9:31; 10:33; 14:21) but also to John the Baptist (1:14) and to the disciples (13:9–12). One can and should read them in terms of both human and divine agency.
52. On Mark's potential indebtedness to Zech. 9–14 throughout the passion account, see Marcus, *Way of the Lord*, 156–59.
53. Ibid., 154. See also Sharyn Dowd, *Prayer, Power, and the Problem of Suffering: Mark 11:22–25 in the Context of Markan Theology*, Society of Biblical Literature Dissertation Series 105 (Atlanta: Scholars Press, 1988), 134; Johnson, "God in Mark," 336–37; Moloney, *Mark*, 288.
54. Moloney, *Mark*, 288. It should be noted that Jesus also promises a reunion with the disciples in Galilee "after I am raised" (14:28).
55. Minor, *Spirituality*, 60.
56. I will explore the theological ramifications of this promise in chapter five.
57. Cf. 13:34, 35, 37.
58. Following Johnson, "God in Mark," 344–45. See also Louis A. Ruprecht, "Mark's Tragic Vision: Gethsemane," *Religion and Literature* 24 (1992): 11–12.
59. Tannehill, "Narrative Christology," 87. On other tensions within the Gethsemane scene see Dowd, *Prayer*, 151–62; and Garrett, *Temptations*, 89–100.
60. So Moloney, *Mark*, 299.
61. Werner H. Kelber, "Mark 14:32–42: Gethsemane: Passion Christology and Discipleship Failure," *Zeitschrift für die neutestamentliche Wissenschaft* 63 (1972): 185.
62. Perhaps implying Jesus' identification with God (cf. 6:50).
63. On the logic of the conviction see Donald H. Juel, "The Function of the Trial of Jesus in Mark's Gospel," *Society of Biblical Literature Seminar Papers* 9 (Missoula, MT: Scholars Press, 1975), 83–104; idem, *Messiah and Temple*, 77–116. Cf. Marcus, *Way of the Lord*, 164–71; idem, "Mark 14:61: 'Are You the Messiah-Son-of-God?'" *Novum Testamentum* 31 (1989): 125–41.
64. Marcus identifies a number of subtler allusions to Psalm 22 (*Way of the Lord*, 180–82) as well as to Isaiah (ibid., 186–96).

65. C. Clifton Black, "Christ Crucified in Paul and in Mark: Reflections on an Intracanonical Conversation," in *Theology and Ethics in Paul and His Interpreters: Essays in Honor of Victor Paul Furnish*, ed. Eugene H. Lovering and Jerry L. Sumney (Nashville: Abingdon, 1996), 199.
66. Tannehill, "Narrative Christology," 84.
67. One sees this perspective, though expressed somewhat differently, at Acts 4:23–31 and 1 Cor. 1:18–31.
68. Contra Kelber, "Mark 14:32–42," 182.
69. Here again I assume an audience loosely familiar with the early Christian kerygma, at least with respect to the claim of a crucified Messiah.
70. Juel, *Mark*, 164.
71. This is the case even if one grounded Mark's transcendent logic in the brief references to vicarious ransom (10:45; 14:24) (Juel, *Mark*, 160; see also Minor, *Spirituality*, 56–57). See, however, the suggestive arguments of Dowd and Malbon, "Significance of Jesus' Death," passim. Cf. Marcus, *Way of the Lord*, 194–95; Mark S. Medley, "Emancipatory Solidarity: The Redemptive Significance of Jesus in Mark," *Perspectives in Religious Studies* 21 (1994): 5–22; Jack Dean Kingsbury, "The Significance of the Cross within Mark's Story," *Interpretation* 47 (1993): 370–79; Barnabas Lindars, "Salvation Proclaimed: VII. Mark X.45: A Ransom for Many," *Expository Times* 93 (1982): 292–95; Garrett, *Temptations*, 104–15.

Chapter Five

1. Rowan Williams, *Why Study the Past? The Quest for the Historical Church* (Grand Rapids: Eerdmans, 2005), 114.
2. Because his white robe (λευκός, 16:5) echoes Jesus' own transfiguration (9:3), and because he knows about Jesus' promise of restoration (14:28), I take the young man to be no normal human and thus call him angelic.
3. Although later scribes added longer endings to Mark's Gospel, I follow the near-unanimous text-critical conclusion that the original ending is 16:8. See Metzger, *Textual Commentary*, 102–6.
4. Matt. 28:1–20; Luke 24:1–53; see also John 20:1–30.
5. I do not treat here the more speculative explanations for Mark 16:8, such that the original ending was lost or that Mark intended to write a more proper ending but was forced, for whatever reason, to end abruptly (e.g., Croy, *Mutilation*, 133–67; Edwards, *Gospel According to Mark*, 501–4). See the brief survey in Corina Combet-Galland, "Qui roulera la peur? Finales d'évangile et figures de lecteur," *Études théologiques et religieuses* 65 (1990): 174–78. Likewise, the possibility of ending an entire narrative with the postpositive γάρ no longer troubles scholars the way it once did. See P. W. van der Horst, "Can a Book End with ΓΑΡ? A Note on Mark xvi. 8," *Journal of Theological Studies* 23 (1972): 121–24; Steven Lynn Cox, *A History and Critique of Scholarship Concerning the Markan Endings* (Lewiston, NY: Edwin Mellen, 1993), 152; cf. Kelly R. Iverson, "A Further Word on Final Γάρ (Mark 16:8)," *Catholic Biblical Quarterly* 68 (2006): 79–94; Charles F. D. Moule, "St. Mark XVI. 8 Once More," *New Testament Studies* 2 (1955): 58–59.
6. David Catchpole, "The Fearful Silence of the Women at the Tomb: A Study in Markan Theology," *Journal of Theology for Southern Africa* 18 (1977): 6–7. See also Hooker, *Mark*, 393; Gerald O' Collins, "The Fearful Silence of Three Women (Mark 16:8c)," *Gregorianum* 69 (1988): 491; and J. Lee Magness, *Sense and Absence: Structure and Suspension in the Ending of Mark's Gospel*, Semeia Studies (Atlanta: Scholars Press, 1986), 100.

7. C. E. B. Cranfield, "St. Mark 16.1–8," *Scottish Journal of Theology* 5 (1952): 293–94. See also Robert H. Smith, "New and Old in Mark 16:1–8," *Concordia Theological Monthly* 43 (1972): 526.

8. GNB, KJV, NAB, NIV, NJB, NKJV, NLT, NRSV, RSV.

9. It is possible to understand the double negative in English—"they said nothing to no one"—in the exact opposite sense: "to no one did they speak nothing." In other words, they did not refrain from speaking to anyone. By translating the indirect object οὐδενὶ as "to anyone," one eliminates this interpretive possibility while also making the English grammar less awkward.

10. So Richard W. Swanson, "'They Said Nothing,'" *Currents in Theology and Mission* 20 (1993): 471; Elizabeth Struthers Malbon, "Fallible Followers: Women and Men in the Gospel of Mark," in *Company of Jesus*, 65; Morna D. Hooker, *Endings: Invitations to Discipleship* (Peabody, MA: Hendrickson, 2003), 21; Moloney, *Mark*, 351–52.

11. Theodore J. Weeden, *Mark—Traditions in Conflict* (Philadelphia: Fortress, 1971), 70–100; idem, "The Heresy That Necessitated Mark's Gospel," in *Interpretation of Mark*, 92–93. Similar polemical interpretations have been forwarded by Werner Kelber, *The Kingdom in Mark: A New Place and a New Time* (Philadelphia: Fortress, 1974); John Dominic Crossan, "Mark and the Relatives of Jesus," *Novum Testamentum* 15 (1973): 81–113; idem, "Empty Tomb and Absent Lord," in *The Passion in Mark: Studies on Mark 14–16*, ed. Werner H. Kelber (Philadelphia: Fortress, 1976), 135–52; William R. Telford, *The Theology of the Gospel of Mark*, New Testament Theology (Cambridge: Cambridge University Press, 1999), 30–54, 137–51. See also Magness, *Sense and Absence*, 91.

12. Weeden, *Mark*, 117.

13. See Weeden, "Heresy," 99.

14. See also the criticisms of Fowler, *Let the Reader Understand*, 256–60; Hanson, *Endangered Promises*, 211–21.

15. Isaac Watts, quoted in Cranfield, "St. Mark 16.1–8," 298.

16. R. H. Lightfoot, *The Gospel Message of St. Mark* (Oxford: Clarendon, 1950), 87.

17. Ibid., 97. See also Catchpole, "Fearful Silence," 7–10; Howard Clark Kee, *Community of the New Age: Studies in Mark's Gospel* (Philadelphia: Westminster, 1977), 68; John R. Donahue, "Jesus as Parable of God in the Gospel of Mark," *Interpretation* 32 (1978): 380–81; C. S. Mann, *Mark: A New Translation with Introduction and Commentary*, Anchor Bible 27 (Garden City, NY: Doubleday, 1986), 662; Magness, *Sense and Absence*, 101; O'Collins, "Fearful Silence," 499–501; see also the more nuanced interpretation of Minor, *Spirituality*, 45–46.

18. Lincoln, "Promise and Failure," 286–87.

19. Ibid., 286. See also Danove, *Rhetoric of Characterization*, 95–96.

20. This view is not as widely held as the others (though it is inferred in Tolbert, *Sowing the Gospel*, 291); but I mention it here to make a larger point about Mark's view of discipleship.

21. See Hisako Kinukawa, "Women Disciples of Jesus (15.40–41; 15.47; 16.1)," in *Feminist Companion to Mark*, 171–90.

22. Tolbert, *Sowing the Gospel*, 291.

23. Malbon, "Fallible Followers," 41–69.

24. Kermode, *Genesis of Secrecy*, 72. See also Frank Kermode, *The Sense of an Ending: Studies in the Theory of Fiction* (London: Oxford University Press, 1966).

25. See Fowler, *Let the Reader Understand*, 230–32.

26. Matt. 28:1–20; Luke 24:1–53.
27. Mark 16:8b–20.
28. In addition to the above interpretations, see the survey in Croy, *Mutilation*, 72–112.
29. Swanson, "'They Said Nothing,'" 472.
30. Following the vast majority of Markan interpreters, I take Mark 16:6–7 to represent the fulfillment of Jesus' promise at 14:28 and not a cloaked reference to the Parousia. So Robert H. Stein, "A Short Note on Mark XIV. 28 and XVI. 7," *New Testament Studies* 20 (1974): 445–52; Croy, *Mutilation*, 102–4; Mann, *Mark*, 669–70; Lincoln, "Promise and Failure," 285; cf. Ernst Lohmeyer, *Galiläa und Jerusalem*, Forschungen zur Religion und Literatur des Alten und Neuen Testaments 52 (Göttingen: Vandenhoeck & Ruprecht, 1936), 10–14.
31. Juel, *Master*, 114–15; see also Moloney, *Mark*, 349; James G. Williams, *Gospel against Parable*, 106.
32. Contra Croy, *Mutilation*, 105.
33. As suggested by Magness, *Sense and Absence*, 115; Lincoln, "Promise and Failure," 292; Kingsbury, *Conflict in Mark*, 112–15; Joel F. Williams, "Literary Approaches to the End of Mark's Gospel," *Journal of the Evangelical Theological Society* 42 (1999): 34.
34. See Juel, *Master*, 116.
35. Blount, "Is the Joke on Us? Mark's Irony, Mark's God, and Mark's Ending," in *Ending of Mark*, 17.
36. Croy, *Mutilation*, 97.
37. The problem has been captured well by Norman R. Petersen, "When Is the End Not the End? Literary Reflections on the Ending of Mark's Narrative," *Interpretation* 34 (1980): 151–66.
38. Lincoln, "Promise and Failure," 290.
39. Tolbert, *Sowing the Gospel*, 288–99.
40. Ibid., 297.
41. See Blount, *Go Preach!* 82–98.
42. For example, Tannehill, "Disciples in Mark," 57; Petersen, "When Is the End?"151–66; Thomas E. Boomershine, "Mark 16:8 and the Apostolic Commission," *Journal of Biblical Literature* 100 (1981): 237; Williamson, *Mark*, 285; Myers, *Binding the Strong Man*, 399–404; Lincoln, "Promise and Failure," 297–98; Combet-Galland, "Qui roulera la peur?" 182, 188; Fowler, *Let the Reader Understand*, 258–59, 262–63; Mary Cotes, "Women, Silence and Fear (Mark 16:8)," in *Women in the Biblical Tradition*, ed. George J. Brooke, Studies in Women and Religion 31 (Lewiston, NY: Edwin Mellen, 1992), 151–66; Paul Danove, *The End of Mark's Story: A Methodological Story*, Biblical Interpretation Series 3 (Leiden: Brill, 1993), 203–30; idem, "The Characterization and Narrative Function of the Women at the Tomb (Mark 15,40–41.47; 16,1–8)," *Biblica* 77 (1996): 397; David J. Hester, "Dramatic Inconclusion: Irony and the Narrative Rhetoric of the Ending of Mark," *Journal for the Study of the New Testament* 57 (1995): 61–86; Blount, *Go Preach!* 185–96; idem, "Is the Joke on Us?" passim; Maria Gemma Victorino, "Mark's Open Ending and Following Jesus on the Way: An Autobiographical Interpretation of the Gospel of Mark," in *The Personal Voice in Biblical Interpretation*, ed. Ingrid Rosa Kitzberger (London: Routledge, 1999), 53–63; Hooker, *Endings*, 23; Sharon H. Ringe, "The Church and the Resurrection: Another Look at the Ending of Mark," in *Literary Encounters with the Reign of God*, ed. Sharon H. Ringe and H. C. Paul Kim (New York: T & T Clark, 2004), 243–44.

43. See Hanson, *Endangered Promises*, 245–46.
44. Blount, "Is the Joke on Us?" 23.
45. Contra Blount, "Is the Joke on Us?" 29–30.
46. A point missed by Kermode, *Genesis*, 125–45; Kingsbury, *Conflict in Mark*, 112–13; O'Collins, "Fearful Silence," 498; Croy, *Mutilation*, 64, 105.
47. Rowan Williams, *Why Study the Past?* 114.
48. On this point I am indebted especially to Brian Blount and Elizabeth Struthers Malbon, both of whom offered insightful feedback to an earlier version of this chapter.

Conclusion

1. Augustine, *Serm.* 52.16. Quoted in Benedict XVI, *Deus caritas est*, 38 (December 25, 2005).
2. We both claim that Mark's Gospel is fundamentally "about God," that Mark's depiction of God is closely connected to Jesus, and that, in Johnson's words, "there is more to God in Mark than God in Jesus" ("God in Mark," 412). My consistent use of Johnson throughout the present work has revealed a number of smaller agreements as well.
3. These categories pertain more to ideological alignment (Johnson, "God in Mark," 242–43) and are therefore not identical to my own categories of invasion and transcendence.
4. Ibid., 381.
5. Ibid., 347.
6. Ibid., 180–82.
7. Hooker, *Mark*, 377.
8. Augustine, *Serm.* 52.16. Quoted in Benedict XVI, *Deus caritas est*, 38 (December 25, 2005).
9. Hanson, *Endangered Promises*, 214–21. See also Matera, *What Are They Saying about Mark?* 41.
10. For example, Weeden, *Mark*; idem, "Heresy"; Tyson, "Blindness of the Disciples."
11. For example, Tannehill, "Disciples in Mark"; Best, *Following Jesus*; idem, "Role of the Disciples"; Petersen, "When Is the End?"
12. Hanson, *Endangered Promises*, 220.
13. Ibid., 246.

Bibliography

Abogunrin, Samuel O. "The Three Variant Accounts of Peter's Call: A Critical and Theological Examination of the Texts." *New Testament Studies* 31 (1985): 587–602.

Abrams, M. H. *The Mirror and the Lamp: Romantic Theory and the Critical Tradition.* New York: Oxford University Press, 1953.

Achtemeier, Paul J. *Mark.* 2nd ed. Proclamation Commentaries. Philadelphia: Fortress, 1986.

Anderson, Hugh. *The Gospel of Mark.* New Century Bible Commentary. 1976. Reprint, Grand Rapids: Eerdmans, 1981.

Anderson, Janice Capel, and Stephen D. Moore, eds. *Mark and Method: New Approaches in Biblical Studies.* Minneapolis: Fortress, 1992.

Austin, J. L. *How to Do Things with Words.* Cambridge: Harvard University Press, 1962.

Bal, Mieke. *Narratology: Introduction to the Theory of Narrative.* 2nd ed. Toronto: University of Toronto Press, 1997.

Bassler, Jouette M. "God (NT)." In *The Anchor Bible Dictionary*, edited by David Noel Freedman, 6:1049–55. 6 vols. New York: Doubleday, 1992.

Beavis, Mary Ann. *Mark's Audience: The Literary and Social Setting of Mark 4:11–12.* Journal for the Study of the New Testament Supplement 33. Sheffield: Sheffield Academic Press, 1989.

Benedict XVI. *Deus caritas est.* December 25, 2005.

Best, Ernest. "The Role of the Disciples in Mark." *New Testament Studies* 23 (1977): 377–401.

———. *Following Jesus: Discipleship in the Gospel of Mark.* Journal for the Study of the New Testament Supplement 4. Sheffield: Journal for the Study of the Old Testament Press, 1981.

Bishop, Jonathan. "*Parabole* and *Parrhesia* in Mark." *Interpretation* 40 (1986): 39–52.

Black, C. Clifton. "Christ Crucified in Paul and in Mark: Reflections on an Intracanonical Conversation." In *Theology and Ethics in Paul and His Interpreters: Essays in Honor of Victor Paul Furnish*, edited by Eugene H. Lovering and Jerry L. Sumney, 184–206. Nashville: Abingdon, 1996.

———. *The Rhetoric of the Gospel: Theological Artistry in the Gospels and Acts.* St. Louis: Chalice, 2001.

———. "The Face Is Familiar—I Just Can't Place It." In *The Ending of Mark and the Ends of God: Essays in Memory of Donald Harrisville Juel*, edited by Beverly Roberts Gaventa and Patrick D. Miller, 33–49. Louisville: Westminster John Knox, 2005.

Blount, Brian K. *Go Preach! Mark's Kingdom Message and the Black Church Today.* Maryknoll, NY: Orbis, 1998.

————. "Is the Joke on Us? Mark's Irony, Mark's God, and Mark's Ending." In *The Ending of Mark and the Ends of God: Essays in Memory of Donald Harrisville Juel*, edited by Beverly Roberts Gaventa and Patrick D. Miller, 15–32. Louisville: Westminster John Knox, 2005.

Boismard, M. É. "Two-Source Hypothesis." In *The Anchor Bible Dictionary*, edited by David Noel Freedman, 6:679–82. 6 vols. New York: Doubleday, 1992.

Boomershine, Thomas E. "Mark 16:8 and the Apostolic Commission." *Journal of Biblical Literature* 100 (1981): 225–39.

Booth, Wayne C. *The Rhetoric of Fiction*. 2nd ed. Chicago: University of Chicago Press, 1983.

Boring, M. Eugene. "Markan Christology: God-Language for Jesus?" *New Testament Studies* 45 (1999): 451–71.

Camery-Hoggatt, Jerry. *Irony in Mark's Gospel: Text and Subtext*. Society for New Testament Studies Monograph Series 72. Cambridge: Cambridge University Press, 1992.

Candler, Peter M., Jr. *Theology, Rhetoric, Manuduction, or Reading Scripture Together on the Path to God*. Grand Rapids: Eerdmans, 2006.

Catchpole, David. "The Fearful Silence of the Women at the Tomb: A Study in Markan Theology." *Journal of Theology for Southern Africa* 18 (1977): 3–10.

Cave, Nick. Introduction to *The Gospel According to Mark*. Edinburgh: Canongate, 1998.

Charlesworth, James H., ed. *The Messiah: Developments in Earliest Judaism and Christianity*. Minneapolis: Fortress, 1992.

Chatman, Seymour. *Story and Discourse: Narrative Structure in Fiction and Film*. Ithaca: Cornell University Press, 1978.

Collins, Adela Yarbro. "Rulers, Divine Men, and Walking on the Water (Mark 6:45–52)." In *Religious Propaganda and Missionary Competition in the New Testament World: Essays Honoring Dieter Georgi*, edited by Lukas Bormann, Kelly Del Tredici, and Angela Standhartinger, 207–27. Leiden: Brill, 1994.

Collins, John J. *The Scepter and the Star: The Messiahs of the Dead Sea Scrolls and Other Ancient Literature*. New York: Doubleday, 1995.

Combet-Galland, Corina. "Qui roulera la peur? Finales d'évangile et figures de lecteur." *Études théologiques et religieuses* 65 (1990): 171–89.

Cotes, Mary. "Women, Silence and Fear (Mark 16:8)." In *Women in the Biblical Tradition*, edited by George J. Brooke, 151–66. Studies in Women and Religion 31. Lewiston, NY: Edwin Mellen, 1992.

Countryman, L. Wm. "How Many Baskets Full? Mark 8:14–21 and the Value of Miracles in Mark." *Catholic Biblical Quarterly* 47 (1985): 643–55.

Cox, Steven Lynn. *A History and Critique of Scholarship Concerning the Markan Endings*. Lewiston, NY: Edwin Mellen, 1993.

Cranfield, C. E. B. "St. Mark 16.1–8." *Scottish Journal of Theology* 5 (1952): 282–98.

Crossan, John Dominic. "Mark and the Relatives of Jesus." *Novum Testamentum* 15 (1973): 81–113.

————. "Empty Tomb and Absent Lord." In *The Passion in Mark: Studies on Mark 14–16*, edited by Werner H. Kelber, 135–52. Philadelphia: Fortress, 1976.

Croy, N. Clayton. *The Mutilation of Mark's Gospel*. Nashville: Abingdon, 2003.

Culler, Jonathan. "Literary Competence." In *Reader-Response Criticism: From Formalism to Post-Structuralism*, edited by Jane P. Tompkins, 101–17. Baltimore: Johns Hopkins University Press, 1980.

Cunningham, Conor. *Genealogy of Nihilism: Philosophies of Nothing and the Difference of Theology*. London: Routledge, 2002.

Dahl, Nils. *Jesus the Christ: The Historical Origins of Christological Doctrine*, edited by Donald H. Juel. Minneapolis: Fortress, 1991.

Danove, Paul. *The End of Mark's Story: A Methodological Story*. Biblical Interpretation Series 3. Leiden: Brill, 1993.

————. "The Characterization and Narrative Function of the Women at the Tomb (Mark 15,40–41.47; 16,1–8)." *Biblica* 77 (1996): 375–97.

————. "The Narrative Function of Mark's Characterization of God." *Novum Testamentum* 43 (2001): 12–30.

————. *The Rhetoric of Characterization of God, Jesus, and Jesus' Disciples in the Gospel of Mark*. Journal for the Study of the New Testament Supplement 290. New York: T & T Clark, 2005.

Das, A. Andrew, and Frank J. Matera, eds. *The Forgotten God: Perspectives in Biblical Theology: Essays in Honor of Paul J. Achtemeier on the Occasion of His Seventy-fifth Birthday*. Louisville: Westminster John Knox, 2002.

de Jonge, Marinus. "Messiah." In *The Anchor Bible Dictionary*, edited by David Noel Freedman, 4:777–88. 6 vols. New York: Doubleday, 1992.

Delorme, Jean. "Text and Context: 'The Gospel' According to Mark 1:14–18." In *Text and Logos: The Humanistic Interpretation of the New Testament*, edited by Theodore W. Jennings Jr., 273–87. Atlanta: Scholars Press, 1990.

Derrett, J. Duncan M. "Ἦσαν γαρ ἁλιεισ (Mk. i 16): Jesus's Fishermen and the Parable of the Net." *Novum Testamentum* 22 (1980): 108–37.

Dewey, Joanna. *Markan Public Debate: Literary Technique, Concentric Structure, and Theology in Mark 2:1–3:6*. Society of Biblical Literature Dissertation Series 48. Chico, CA: Scholars Press, 1980.

————. "Point of View and the Disciples in Mark." Pages 97–106 in *Society of Biblical Literature Seminar Papers* 21. Missoula, MT: Scholars Press, 1982.

————. "The Literary Structure of the Controversy Stories in Mark 2:1–3:6." In *The Interpretation of Mark*, edited by William R. Telford, 141–51. Edinburgh: T & T Clark, 1995. Reprint from *Journal of Biblical Literature* 92 (1973): 394–401.

————. "'Let Them Renounce Themselves and Take Up Their Cross': A Feminist Reading of Mark 8:34 in Mark's Social and Narrative World." In *A Feminist Companion to Mark*, edited by Amy-Jill Levine, 23–36. Cleveland: Pilgrim Press, 2001.

Donahue, John R. "Jesus as Parable of God in the Gospel of Mark." *Interpretation* 32 (1978): 369–86.

————. "A Neglected Factor in the Theology of Mark." *Journal of Biblical Literature* 101 (1982): 562–94.

————. *The Theology and Setting of Discipleship in the Gospel of Mark*. Milwaukee: Marquette University Press, 1983.

————. "The Revelation of God in the Gospel of Mark." In *Modern Biblical Scholarship: Its Impact on Theology and Proclamation*, edited by Francis A. Eigo, 157–83. Villanova: Villanova University Press, 1984.

Donahue, John R., and Daniel J. Harrington. *The Gospel of Mark*. Sacra pagina 2. Collegeville, MN: Liturgical Press, 2002.

Dowd, Sharyn. *Prayer, Power, and the Problem of Suffering: Mark 11:22–25 in the Context of Markan Theology*. Society of Biblical Literature Dissertation Series 105. Atlanta: Scholars Press, 1988.

Dowd, Sharyn, and Elizabeth Struthers Malbon. "The Significance of Jesus' Death in Mark: Narrative Context and Authorial Audience." *Journal of Biblical Literature* 125 (2006): 271–97.

Driggers, Ira Brent. "The Politics of Divine Presence: Temple as Locus of Conflict in the Gospel of Mark." Forthcoming in *Biblical Interpretation: A Journal of Contemporary Approaches* 15 (2007): 270–90.

Dunn, James D. G. "'Are You the Messiah?': Is the Crux of Mark 14:61–62 Resolvable?" In *Christology, Controversy and Community: New Testament Essays in Honour of David R. Catchpole*, edited by David G. Horrell and Christopher M. Tuckett, 1–22. Novum Testamentum Supplement 99. Leiden: Brill, 2000.

Edwards, James R. *The Gospel according to Mark*. Pillar New Testament Commentary. Grand Rapids: Eerdmans, 2002.

Elliott, J. K. "Mark and the Teaching of Jesus: An Examination of ΛΟΓΟΣ and ΕΥΑΓΓΕΛΙΟΝ." In *Sayings of Jesus: Canonical and Non-canonical: Essays in Honor of Tjitze Baarda*, edited by William L. Petersen, Johan S. Vos, and Henk J. de Jonge, 37–45. Novum Testamentum Supplement 89. Leiden: Brill, 1997.

English, Donald. *The Message of Mark*. Downers Grove, IL: InterVarsity Press, 1992.

Evans, Craig A. "A Note on the Function of Isaiah, VI 9–10 in Mark, IV." *Revue biblique* 88 (1981): 234–35.

———. "On the Isaianic Background of the Sower Parable." *Catholic Biblical Quarterly* 47 (1985): 464–68.

Fay, Greg. "Introduction to Incomprehension: The Literary Structure of Mark 4:1–34." *Catholic Biblical Quarterly* 51 (1989): 65–81.

Fish, Stanley. *Is There a Text in This Class? The Authority of Interpretive Communities*. Cambridge: Harvard University Press, 1980.

Fowler, Robert. *Loaves and Fishes: The Function of the Feeding Stories in the Gospel of Mark*. Society of Biblical Literature Dissertation Series 54. Chico, CA: Scholars Press, 1981.

———. *Let the Reader Understand: Reader-Response Criticism and the Gospel of Mark*. Minneapolis: Fortress, 1991.

Freedman, David Noel, ed. *The Anchor Bible Dictionary*. 6 vols. New York: Doubleday, 1992.

Fretheim, Terence E. *Exodus*. Interpretation: A Bible Commentary for Teaching and Preaching. Louisville: John Knox, 1991.

Gadamer, Hans-Georg. *Truth and Method*. 3rd ed. Translated by Joel Weinsheimer and Donald G. Marshall. New York: Continuum, 1993.

Gamble, Harry Y. *Books and Readers in the Early Church: A History of Early Christian Texts*. New Haven: Yale University Press, 1995.

Garrett, Susan R. *The Temptations of Jesus in Mark's Gospel*. Grand Rapids: Eerdmans, 1998.

Gaventa, Beverly Roberts, and Patrick D. Miller, eds. *The Ending of Mark and the Ends of God: Essays in Memory of Donald Harrisville Juel*. Louisville: Westminster John Knox, 2005.

Genette, Gérard. *Narrative Discourse: An Essay in Method*. Translated by Jane E. Lewin. Ithaca, NY: Cornell University Press, 1980.

Giblin, Charles Homer. "The Beginning of the Ongoing Gospel (Mk 1,2–16,8)." In *The Four Gospels 1992: Festschrift Frans Neirynck*, edited by F. Van Segbroeck, C. M. Tuckett, G. van Belle, and J. Verheyden, 2:975–85. 3 vols. Bibliotheca ephemeridum theologicarum lovaniensium 100. Leuven: Leuven University Press, 1992.

Gibson, Jeffrey B. "The Rebuke of the Disciples in Mark 8:14–21." *Journal for the Study of the New Testament* 27 (1986): 31–47.

Goulder, Michael D. "Those Outside (Mk. 4:10–12)." *Novum Testamentum* 33 (1991): 289–302.

Guelich, Robert A. *Mark 1–8:26.* Word Biblical Commentary 34A. Dallas: Word, 1989.

Gurtner, Daniel M. "LXX Syntax and the Identity of the NT Veil." *Novum Testamentum* 47 (2005): 344–53.

Hahn, Ferdinand. "The Confession of the One God in the New Testament." *Horizons in Biblical Theology* 2 (1980): 69–84.

Hamerton-Kelly, Robert G. *The Gospel and the Sacred: Poetics of Violence in Mark.* Minneapolis: Fortress, 1994.

Hanson, James S. *The Endangered Promises: Conflict in Mark.* Society of Biblical Literature Dissertation Series 171. Atlanta: Society of Biblical Literature, 2001.

Harrisville, Roy A. *Fracture: The Cross as Irreconcilable in the Language and Thought of the Biblical Writers.* Grand Rapids: Eerdmans, 2006.

Havelock, Eric A. *The Literate Revolution in Greece and Its Cultural Consequences.* Princeton: Princeton University Press, 1982.

Hays, Richard B. *Echoes of Scripture in the Letters of Paul.* New Haven: Yale University Press, 1989.

Henderson, Suzanne Watts. "'Concerning the Loaves': Comprehending Incomprehension in Mark 6:45–52." *Journal for the Study of the New Testament* 83 (2001): 3–26.

Hester, David J. "Dramatic Inconclusion: Irony and the Narrative Rhetoric of the Ending of Mark." *Journal for the Study of the New Testament* 57 (1995): 61–86.

Hooker, Morna D. *The Gospel According to Saint Mark.* Black's New Testament Commentaries. Peabody, MA: Hendrickson, 1991.

———. *Endings: Invitations to Discipleship.* Peabody, MA: Hendrickson, 2003.

Horsley, Richard A. *Hearing the Whole Story: The Politics of Plot in Mark's Gospel.* Louisville: Westminster John Knox, 2001.

Horst, P. W. van der. "Can a Book End with ΓΑΡ? A Note on Mark xvi. 8." *Journal of Theological Studies* 23 (1972): 121–24.

Humphreys, W. Lee. *The Character of God in the Book of Genesis: A Narrative Appraisal.* Louisville: Westminster John Knox, 2001.

Iser, Wolfgang. *The Implied Reader: Patterns of Communication in Prose Fiction from Bunyan to Beckett.* Baltimore: Johns Hopkins University Press, 1974.

———. *The Act of Reading: A Theory of Aesthetic Response.* Baltimore: Johns Hopkins University Press, 1978.

Iverson, Kelly R. "A Further Word on Final Γάρ (Mark 16:8)." *Catholic Biblical Quarterly* 68 (2006): 79–94.

Johnson, Philip Reubin. "God in Mark: The Narrative Function of God as a Character in the Gospel of Mark." PhD diss., Luther Seminary, 2000.

Juel, Donald H. "The Function of the Trial of Jesus in Mark's Gospel." Pages 83–104 in vol. 2 of the *Society of Biblical Literature Seminar Papers* 9. 2 vols. Missoula, MT: Scholars Press, 1975.

———. *Messiah and Temple: The Trial of Jesus in the Gospel of Mark.* Society of Biblical Literature Dissertation Series 31. Missoula, MT: Scholars Press, 1977.

———. *Messianic Exegesis: Christological Interpretation of the Old Testament in Early Christianity.* Philadelphia: Fortress, 1988.

———. *A Master of Surprise: Mark Interpreted.* Minneapolis: Fortress, 1994.

———. *The Gospel of Mark.* Interpreting Biblical Texts. Nashville: Abingdon, 1999.

Keck, Leander E. "The Introduction to Mark's Gospel." *New Testament Studies* 12 (1966): 352–70.

Kee, Howard Clark. *Community of the New Age: Studies in Mark's Gospel.* Philadelphia: Westminster, 1977.

Kelber, Werner. "Mark 14:32–42: Gethsemane: Passion Christology and Discipleship Failure," *Zeitschrift für die neutestamentliche Wissenschaft* 63 (1972): 166–87.

———. *The Kingdom in Mark: A New Place and a New Time.* Philadelphia: Fortress, 1974.

Keller, Joseph. "Jesus and the Critics: A Logo-Critical Analysis of the Marcan Confrontation." *Interpretation* 40 (1986): 29–38.

Kermode, Frank. *The Sense of an Ending: Studies in the Theory of Fiction.* London: Oxford University Press, 1966.

———. *The Genesis of Secrecy: On the Interpretation of Narrative.* Cambridge: Harvard University Press, 1979.

Kingsbury, Jack Dean. *The Christology of Mark's Gospel.* Philadelphia: Fortress, 1983.

———. *Conflict in Mark: Jesus, Authorities, Disciples.* Minneapolis: Fortress, 1989.

———. "The Significance of the Cross within Mark's Story." *Interpretation* 47 (1993): 370–79.

———. "'God' within the Narrative World of Mark." In *The Forgotten God: Perspectives in Biblical Theology: Essays in Honor of Paul J. Achtemeier on the Occasion of His Seventy-fifth Birthday*, edited by A. Andrew Das and Frank J. Matera, 75–88. Louisville: Westminster John Knox, 2002.

Kinukawa, Hisako. "Women Disciples of Jesus (15.40–41; 15.47; 16.1)." In *A Feminist Companion to Mark*, edited by Amy-Jill Levine, 171–90. Cleveland: Pilgrim Press, 2001.

Levine, Amy-Jill, ed. *A Feminist Companion to Mark.* Cleveland: Pilgrim Press, 2001.

Lightfoot, R. H. *The Gospel Message of St. Mark.* Oxford: Clarendon, 1950.

Lincoln, Andrew T. "The Promise and the Failure: Mark 16:7, 8." *Journal of Biblical Literature* 108 (1989): 283–300.

Lindars, Barnabas. "Salvation Proclaimed: VII. Mark X.45: A Ransom for Many." *Expository Times* 93 (1982): 292–95.

Lohmeyer, Ernst. *Galiläa und Jerusalem.* Forschungen zur Religion und Literatur des Alten und Neuen Testaments 52. Göttingen: Vandenhoeck & Ruprecht, 1936.

Lull, David J. "Interpreting Mark's Story of Jesus' Death: Toward a Theology of Suffering." Pages 1–12 of *Society of Biblical Literature Seminar Papers* 24. Atlanta: Scholars Press, 1985.

Madigan, Kevin. "Ancient and High-Medieval Interpretations of Jesus in Gethsemane: Some Reflections on Tradition and Continuity in Christian Thought." *Harvard Theological Review* 88 (1995): 157–73.

Magness, J. Lee. *Sense and Absence: Structure and Suspension in the Ending of Mark's Gospel.* Semeia Studies. Atlanta: Scholars Press, 1986.

Malbon, Elizabeth Struthers. "Echoes and Foreshadowings in Mark 4–8: Reading and Rereading." *Journal of Biblical Literature* 112 (1993): 211–30.

———. *In the Company of Jesus: Characters in Mark's Gospel.* Louisville: Westminster John Knox, 2000.

Mann, C. S. *Mark: A New Translation with Introduction and Commentary.* Anchor Bible 27. Garden City, NY: Doubleday, 1986.

Marcus, Joel. "Mark 4:10–12 and Marcan Epistemology." *Journal of Biblical Literature* 103 (1984): 557–74.

———. "Mark 14:61: 'Are You the Messiah-Son-of-God?'" *Novum Testamentum* 31 (1989): 125–41.

———. *The Way of the Lord: Christological Exegesis of the Old Testament in the Gospel of Mark.* Louisville: Westminster John Knox, 1992.

———. "A Note on Markan Optics," *New Testament Studies* 45 (1999): 250–56.

———. *Mark 1–8.* Anchor Bible 27. New York: Doubleday, 2000.

Marshall, Christopher D. *Faith as a Theme in Mark's Narrative.* Society for New Testament Studies Monograph Series 64. Cambridge: Cambridge University Press, 1989.

Matera, Frank. *What Are They Saying about Mark?* New York: Paulist Press, 1987.

———. "The Prologue as the Interpretive Key to Mark's Gospel." *Journal for the Study of the New Testament* 34 (1988): 3–20.

Mauser, Ulrich. *Christ in the Wilderness: The Wilderness Theme in the Second Gospel and Its Basis in the Biblical Tradition.* Studies in Biblical Theology 1/39. London: SCM, 1963.

Mays, James L. "Exposition of Mark 8:27–9:1." *Interpretation* 30 (1976): 174–78.

Medley, Mark S. "Emancipatory Solidarity: The Redemptive Significance of Jesus in Mark." *Perspectives in Religious Studies* 21 (1994): 5–22.

Metzger, Bruce M. *A Textual Commentary on the Greek New Testament.* 2nd ed. Stuttgart: Deutsche Bibelgesellschaft, 1994.

Milavec, Aaron A. "Mark's Parable of the Wicked Husbandmen as Reaffirming God's Predilection for Israel." *Journal of Ecumenical Studies* 26 (1989): 289–312.

Minor, Mitzi. *The Spirituality of Mark: Responding to God.* Louisville: Westminster John Knox, 1996.

Moloney, Francis J. *The Gospel of Mark: A Commentary.* Peabody, MA: Hendrickson, 2002.

Moule, Charles F. D. "St. Mark XVI. 8 Once More." *New Testament Studies* 2 (1955): 58–59.

Myers, Ched. *Binding the Strong Man: A Political Reading of Mark's Story of Jesus.* Maryknoll, NY: Orbis, 1988.

No, Kisun. "The Narrative Function of God in the Gospel of Mark." PhD diss., Southern Baptist Theological Seminary, 1999.

O'Collins, Gerald. "The Fearful Silence of Three Women (Mark 16:8c)," *Gregorianum* 69 (1988): 489–503.

Ong, Walter. *Orality and Literacy: The Technologizing of the Word.* London: Methuen, 1982.

Perkins, Pheme. "God in the New Testament: Preliminary Soundings." *Theology Today* 42 (1985): 332–41.

Perrin, Norman. "Towards an Interpretation of the Gospel of Mark." In *Christology and a Modern Pilgrimage: A Discussion with Norman Perrin*, edited by Hans Dieter Betz, 1–78. Claremont: New Testament Colloquium, 1971.

———. "The Interpretation of the Gospel of Mark," *Interpretation* 30 (1976): 115–24.

Petersen, Norman R. "Point of View in Mark's Narrative." *Semeia* 12 (1978): 97–121.

———. "When Is the End Not the End? Literary Reflections on the Ending of Mark's Narrative." *Interpretation* 34 (1980): 151–66.

Plato. *Phaedrus.* Translated by A. Nehmas and P. Woodruff. Indianapolis: Hackett, 1995.

Powell, Mark Allan. *What Is Narrative Criticism?* Minneapolis: Fortress, 1990.

Quesnell, Quentin. *The Mind of Mark: Interpretation and Method through the Exegesis of Mark 6, 52.* Rome: Pontifical Biblical Institute Press, 1969.

Reumann, John. "Mark 1:14–20." *Interpretation* 32 (1978): 405–10.

Rhoads, David. *Reading Mark: Engaging the Gospel.* Minneapolis: Fortress, 2004.

Rhoads, David, Joanna Dewey, and Donald Michie. *Mark as Story: An Introduction to the Narrative of a Gospel.* 2nd ed. Minneapolis: Fortress, 1999.

Rimmon-Kenan, Shlomith. *Narrative Fiction: Contemporary Poetics.* London: Routledge, 1989.

Ringe, Sharon H. "The Church and the Resurrection: Another Look at the Ending of Mark." In *Literary Encounters with the Reign of God,* edited by Sharon H. Ringe and H. C. Paul Kim, 235–46. New York: T & T Clark, 2004.

Ringe, Sharon H., and H. C. Paul Kim, eds. *Literary Encounters with the Reign of God.* New York: T & T Clark, 2004.

Robinson, James M. *The Problem of History in Mark.* Studies in Biblical Theology 1/21. Naperville, IL: Allenson, 1957.

Ruprecht, Louis A., Jr. "Mark's Tragic Vision: Gethsemane." *Religion and Literature* 24 (1992): 1–25.

Sankey, P. J. "Promise and Fulfilment: Reader-Response to Mark 1.1–15." *Journal for the Study of the New Testament* 58 (1995): 3–18.

Schweizer, Eduard. *The Good News According to Mark.* Translated by Donald H. Madvig. Atlanta: John Knox, 1970.

———. "The Portrayal of the Life of Faith in the Gospel of Mark." *Interpretation* 32 (1978): 387–99.

Scroggs, Robin, and Kent I. Groff. "Baptism in Mark: Dying and Rising with Christ." *Journal of Biblical Literature* 92 (1973): 531–48.

Shiner, Whitney. *Follow Me! Disciples in Markan Rhetoric.* Society of Biblical Literature Dissertation Series 145. Atlanta: Scholars Press, 1995.

———. *Proclaiming the Gospel: First-Century Performance of Mark.* Harrisburg: Trinity Press International, 2003.

———. "Creating the Kingdom: The Performance of Mark as Revelatory Event." In *Literary Encounters with the Reign of God,* edited by Sharon H. Ringe and H. C. Paul Kim, 194–212. New York: T & T Clark, 2004.

Skinner, Matthew L. "Denying Self, Bearing a Cross, and Following Jesus: Unpacking the Imperatives of Mark 8:34." *Word and World* 23 (2003): 321–31.

Smith, Charles W. F. "Fishers of Men: Footnotes on a Gospel Figure." *Harvard Theological Review* 52 (1959): 187–203.

Smith, Robert H. "New and Old in Mark 16:1–8." *Concordia Theological Monthly* 43 (1972): 518–27.

Stein, Robert H. "A Short Note on Mark XIV. 28 and XVI. 7." *New Testament Studies* 20 (1974): 445–52.

Stock, Augustine. "Hinge Transitions in Mark's Gospel. " *Biblical Theology Bulletin* 15 (1985): 27–31.

Swanson, Richard W. "'They Said Nothing.'" *Currents in Theology and Mission* 20 (1993): 471–78.

Tannehill, Robert C. "The Gospel of Mark as Narrative Christology." *Semeia* 16 (1979): 57–95.

———. "The Disciples in Mark: The Function of a Narrative Role." In *The Interpretation of Mark,* edited by William R. Telford, 169–95. Edinburgh: T & T Clark, 1995. Reprint from *Journal of Religion* 57 (1977): 386–405.

Telford, William R. *The Theology of the Gospel of Mark.* New Testament Theology. Cambridge: Cambridge University Press, 1999.

———, ed. *The Interpretation of Mark.* Edinburgh: T & T Clark, 1995.

Thomas, John Christopher. "Discipleship in Mark's Gospel." In *Faces of Renewal: Studies in Honor of Stanley M. Horton Presented on His 70ᵗʰ Birthday*, edited by Paul Elbert, 64–80. Peabody, MA: Hendrickson, 1988.

Thompson, Marianne Meye. *The Promise of the Father: Jesus and God in the New Testament*. Louisville: Westminster John Knox, 2000.

———. *The God of the Gospel of John*. Grand Rapids: Eerdmans, 2001.

Tolbert, Mary Ann. *Sowing the Gospel: Mark's World in Literary-Historical Perspective*. Minneapolis: Fortress, 1989.

Tompkins, Jane P. "The Reader in History: The Changing Shape of Reader Response." In *Reader-Response Criticism: From Formalism to Post-Structuralism*, edited by Jane P. Tompkins, 201–32. Baltimore: Johns Hopkins University Press, 1980.

———, ed. *Reader-Response Criticism: From Formalism to Post-Structuralism*. Baltimore: Johns Hopkins University Press, 1980.

Trakatellis, Demetrios. "'Ἀκολούθει μοι/Follow me' (Mk 2.14): Discipleship and Priesthood." *Greek Orthodox Theological Review* 30 (1985): 271–85.

Tyson, Joseph B. "The Blindness of the Disciples in Mark." *Journal of Biblical Literature* 80 (1961): 261–68.

Ulansey, David. "The Heavenly Veil Torn: Mark's Cosmic *Inclusio*." *Journal of Biblical Literature* 110 (1991): 123–25.

Via, Dan O. *The Ethics of Mark's Gospel: In the Middle of Time*. Philadelphia: Fortress, 1985.

Victorino, Maria Gemma. "Mark's Open Ending and Following Jesus on the Way: An Autobiographical Interpretation of the Gospel of Mark." In *The Personal Voice in Biblical Interpretation*, edited by Ingrid Rosa Kitzberger, 53–63. London: Routledge, 1999.

Weeden, Theodore J. *Mark—Traditions in Conflict*. Philadelphia: Fortress, 1971.

———. "The Heresy That Necessitated Mark's Gospel." In *The Interpretation of Mark*, edited by William R. Telford, 89–104. Edinburgh: T & T Clark, 1995. Reprint from *Zeitschrift für die neutestamentliche Wissenschaft* 59 (1968): 145–58.

Williams, James G. *Gospel against Parable: Mark's Language of Mystery*. Bible and Literature Series 12. Sheffield: Almond, 1985.

Williams, Joel F. "Literary Approaches to the End of Mark's Gospel." *Journal of the Evangelical Theological Society* 42 (1999): 21–35.

Williams, Rowan. *Why Study the Past? The Quest for the Historical Church*. Grand Rapids: Eerdmans, 2005.

Williamson, Lamar, Jr. *Mark*. Interpretation: A Bible Commentary for Teaching and Preaching. Atlanta: John Knox, 1983.

Wilson, Patrick J., and Beverly Roberts Gaventa. "Preaching as the Re-reading of Scripture." *Interpretation* 52 (1998): 392–404.

Wuellner, Wilhelm H. *The Meaning of "Fishers of Men."* New Testament Library. Philadelphia: Westminster, 1967.

Scripture Index

Author Index

Ulansey, David, 110n13

van der Horst, P. W., 122n5
Via, Dan O., 20, 112n37, 114nn28, 40
Victorino, Maria Gemma, 124n42

Watts, Isaac, 88
Weeden, Theodore J., 88, 121n44,
  123nn11–13; 125n10

Williams, James G., 112nn30, 37;
  115n18, 120n25, 124n31
Williams, Joel F., 124n33
Williams, Rowan, 85, 97, 122n1
Williamson, Lamar, 28, 108n12, 112n2,
  124n42
Wilson, Patrick J., 108n17
Wuellner, Wilhelm H., 114nn29,
  31

Following God through Ma

50995